SOUTHERN LITERARY STUDIES
Fred Hobson, *Editor*

Eudora Welty and Virginia Woolf

Eudora Welty and

Virginia Woolf

Gender, Genre, and Influence

SUZAN HARRISON

Louisiana State University Press

Baton Rouge and London

Designer: Barbara Werden
Typeface: Bembo
Typesetter: Impressions Book and Journal Services, Inc.
Printer and binder: Thomson-Shore, Inc.

Library of Congress Cataloging-in-Publication Data

Harrison, Suzan, 1956–
    Eudora Welty and Virginia Woolf : gender, genre, and influence /
Suzan Harrison.
        p.   cm. — (Southern literary studies)
    Includes bibliographical references and index.
    ISBN 0-8071-2095-2 (cl : alk. paper)
    1. Welty, Eudora, 1909– —Knowledge—Literature.   2. Women and
literature—Southern States—History—20th century.   3. Woolf,
Virginia, 1882–1941—Influence.   4. American fiction—English
influences.   5. Literary form.   I. Title.   II. Series.
PS3545.E6Z695   1996
813'.52—dc20   96-30238
                                                              CIP

Chapter I first appeared, in somewhat different form, as "The Other Way to Live: Gender and
Selfhood in *Delta Wedding* and *The Golden Apples,*" *Mississippi Quarterly,* XLIV (1990–91), 49–68,
and is used by permission. Excerpts from *One Writer's Beginnings* by Eudora Welty. Copyright ©
1983, 1984 by Eudora Welty. Reprinted by permission of Harvard University Press.

To Sterling Judd McKean

CONTENTS

ACKNOWLEDGMENTS

I could not have completed this book were it not for the generous assistance of many people. First, I wish to thank Eudora Welty for the pleasure and vision her fiction has offered to me and many others. I thank Anne Rowe for first introducing me to Eudora Welty's fiction. I am especially grateful to Louis D. Rubin, Jr., Doris Betts, Charles Edge, Howard Harper, Trudier Harris, and George Lensing, whose patient advice and guidance helped me compose the first drafts of this project and whose example taught me much about the pleasures of reading, teaching, and writing.

I am indebted to the many knowledgeable and helpful people working in the libraries of the University of North Carolina, the McKeldin Library of the University of Maryland, and the William Cobb library of Eckerd College. Special thanks go to Russell Bailey for handling innumerable interlibrary loans with never a word of complaint.

Special thanks go also to the supportive community of faculty, students, and staff at Eckerd College. The college provided research grants for this project, while my colleagues—especially Bill Kelly, Carolyn Johnston, and George Meese—kept up a constant flow of much-needed encouragement and humor. The assistance provided by Louisiana State University Press has also been invaluable, especially John Easterly's and Catherine Landry's attentive support. Wendy Jacobs was a thorough and perceptive copyeditor.

My debt to the communities of Welty and Woolf scholars is obvious

throughout this study, and I owe special gratitude to Ruth M. Vande Kieft, Michael Kreyling, Peggy Whitman Prenshaw, and Louise Westling, whose scholarship on southern literature has helped to shape my reading of Welty's fiction. In addition, I am indebted to the many feminist writers whose work has challenged me and taught me new ways of reading, including Hélène Cixous, Carolyn Heilbrun, Toril Moi, Diane Price Herndl, and Patricia Yaeger.

Finally, I wish to thank my parents for their many ways of encouraging me and Judd McKean for his unflagging faith and support.

ABBREVIATIONS

C	*Conversations with Eudora Welty*
CE	*Collected Essays of Virginia Woolf*
DW	*Delta Wedding*
E	*The Eye of the Story: Selected Essays and Reviews*
GA	*The Golden Apples*
LB	*Losing Battles*
O	*Orlando*
OD	*The Optimist's Daughter*
OWB	*One Writer's Beginnings*
RB	*The Robber Bridegroom*
ROO	*A Room of One's Own*
TL	*To the Lighthouse*
W	*The Waves*
WD	*A Writer's Diary*

Eudora Welty and Virginia Woolf

INTRODUCTION
"A Sweet Devouring"

T
HE pleasures of reading," writes Eudora Welty, are "like those of a
Christmas cake, a sweet devouring" (*E*, 281). In "A Sweet Devouring," an essay in *The Eye of the Story*, Welty describes her childhood
reading, and what impresses the reader most is her vivid memory of
these works: she describes plot details from *Five Little Peppers* and names
the characters from "The Camp Fire Girls" series as vividly as if she had
read them last week. Almost every page of her literary autobiography,
One Writer's Beginnings, testifies to Welty's insatiable appetite, her "devouring wish to read" (*OWB*, 30). That Welty loves to read, that she
remembers in detail what she reads, and that what she reads is transformed by her imagination and colors her writing, is obvious in such
works as *The Robber Bridegroom*, with its mixture of fairy tale and legend,
and *The Golden Apples*, permeated with classical mythology and the poetry of W. B. Yeats.

Virginia Woolf is one of the authors whose writing Welty has devoured with obvious pleasure. Though Welty does not mention Woolf
in "A Sweet Devouring," two other essays in *The Eye of the Story*—a
review of Woolf's essay collection *Granite and Rainbow*, and a review of
The Letters of Virginia Woolf, Volume II—illustrate Welty's keen, perceptive, and lifelong interest in Woolf's writing, as do her 1944 review of
Woolf's *"A Haunted House" and Other Short Stories* and the foreword she
wrote for a 1981 edition of Woolf's *To the Lighthouse*.[1] Woolf is one of

---

1. Welty's review of *Granite and Rainbow* was published originally in the *New York*

the writers—along with William Faulkner, Elizabeth Bowen, Jane Austen, and Anton Chekhov—whom Welty mentions often in essays and
interviews, and whom she identifies as important to her own development as a writer. In a 1972 *Paris Review* interview, Welty describes the
excitement and enchantment she experienced in her first encounter with
Woolf's fiction: "[Virginia Woolf] was the one who opened the door.
When I read *To the Lighthouse,* I felt, Heavens, *what is this?* I was so excited
by the experience I couldn't sleep or eat. I've read it many times since"
(*C,* 75).

In her review of *Granite and Rainbow,* Welty describes Woolf's importance to the novel as a genre: "The novel, of course, was never to be
the same after the day she started work on it. As novel succeeded novel
she proceeded to break, in turn, each mold of her own" (*E,* 192). More
specifically, Welty's novels would not be the same had Woolf not "opened
the door." If, as Woolf claims, "books continue each other" (*ROO,* 84),
then Welty's books have continued Woolf's imaginative experiments in
narrative structure and content. Indeed, Welty has, in turn, broken each
mold of *her* own.

When I first read Eudora Welty's fiction, I was struck immediately by
her works' affinity with Woolf's novels. The famous passage from *To the
Lighthouse* used so often to describe Woolf's narrative voice and vision
applies equally well to Welty's: "Beautiful and bright it should be on the
surface, feathery and evanescent, one colour melting into another like
the colours on a butterfly's wing; but beneath the fabric must be clamped
together with bolts of iron. It was to be a thing you could ruffle with
your breath; and a thing you could not dislodge with a team of horses"
(*TL,* 255). Welty herself, in a foreword to *To the Lighthouse,* compares
this description of Lily Briscoe's ideal painting to Woolf's own art: "By
no coincidence [these words] come as close as we could ask to a description of the novel." This description is, in fact, very similar to the qualities
of Welty's style that Louis D. Rubin, Jr., describes in *The Faraway Country:
Writers of the Modern South:* "Shimmering, hovering, elusive, fanciful,
fastening on little things. . . . Like the hummingbirds that appear fre-

---

Times Book Review, September 21, 1958. The review of Volume II of *The Letters of Virginia
Woolf* appeared in the *New York Times Book Review,* November 14, 1976.

quently in her stories, it darts here and there, never quite coming to rest, tirelessly invoking light, color, the variety of experience. . . . [It] is also quite muscular, and its elusive, hovering quality is never vague or soft." [2]

As I read more of Welty's fiction, I discovered that the resemblance went beyond a similarity of temperament and surfaces. The two writers share central symbols and motifs: butterflies, water, sun, trees, houses, birds. They experiment with narrative structures and with the novel as a genre in related ways, often to explore similar situations and ideas. Robert Penn Warren's often-quoted description of Welty's primary theme as "love and separateness" could also describe the central issue in many of Virginia Woolf's works; death and absence lie at the center of many Woolf and Welty novels that ostensibly explore the connections— familial, sexual, social—among human beings. [3] Their novels seek out the private realities lying beneath the social fabric and foreground the tension between the two realms. Both writers explore the social and private worlds of women, and both have created female characters— mothers, widows, spinsters—who are artists of one sort or another struggling to find some outlet for their artistic impulses in the circumscribed world permitted to women. The strategies these characters use to construct and order meaning, as well as the ways these two authors' novels construct and order meaning, suggest a shared epistemology as well.

Other readers have noticed the qualities Eudora Welty's fiction shares with Virginia Woolf's. As early as 1946 John Crowe Ransom mentioned this resemblance in his review of *Delta Wedding:* "Miss Welty in her present phase resembles Virginia Woolf more than does any novelist of my acquaintance; the Fairchilds' wedding is the perfect analogue for *Mrs. Dalloway's* party." But Ransom does not pursue this connection, saying, "I am sure the resemblance is fortuitous. Miss Welty's prose, like her people, is her own." Discussing *Delta Wedding,* two of the most sensitive and valuable book-length studies of Welty's fiction mention Woolf's *To the Lighthouse.* Ruth Vande Kieft notes Ellen Fairchild's similarity to

2. Eudora Welty, Foreword to *To the Lighthouse,* by Virginia Woolf (New York, 1981), xii; Louis D. Rubin, Jr., *The Faraway Country: Writers of the Modern South* (Seattle, 1963), 133–34.

3. Robert Penn Warren, "The Love and Separateness in Miss Welty," *Kenyon Review,* VI (1944), 245.

Woolf's Mrs. Ramsay but does not elaborate upon the resemblance between the two characters. Michael Kreyling discusses themes and concerns shared by *To the Lighthouse* and *The Optimist's Daughter*, focusing on
the importance in each novel of "the idea of distance, whether the distance is created by the passing of time or by the gulf between the self
and the public role, self and society, self and loved one, and self and the
truth." Although his discussion is illuminating, Kreyling does not examine the nature of the relationship between the two works, claiming
merely, "The notion of affinity between writers [is] too deeply rooted
and complex for the term *influence*." [4]

In *Author and Agent,* his study of the correspondence between Eudora
Welty and Diarmuid Russell, Kreyling is more specific about the form
of influence that Woolf's fiction had on Welty's development of her tal-
ents as a novelist. He notes that Welty reviewed Woolf's posthumous
collection of stories, *"A Haunted House" and Other Stories,* in the spring
of 1944, while she was in the process of transforming her short story
"The Delta Cousins" into her first full novel, *Delta Wedding*. Kreyling
comments, "Welty's review of the posthumous work is significant for its
timing; just in the hiatus between the completion of a long story that
seemed to require either serious cutting or recasting as a novel, Welty
was brought back to a writer whose fiction had 'opened the door.' . . .
When 'The Delta Cousins' next appears, it is already in the process of
becoming a particular kind of novel, one connected coincidentally as
well as substantially to Welty's rereading of Woolf in the spring of 1944." [5]

Kreyling goes on to speculate that Woolf's work offered Welty both
an imaginative model and a justification for her own "obscurity." He
says, "The obscurity that Welty had been exploring and exploiting in
her own work seemed to find its counterpart in Woolf's successful use
of the 'remove,' the technical means by which she achieved the essential
relationship between reader and author in her fiction." [6]

4. John Crowe Ransom, "Delta Fiction," *Kenyon Review,* VIII (1946), 504; Ruth
Vande Kieft, *Eudora Welty* (rev. ed.; Boston, 1987), 76; Michael Kreyling, *Eudora Welty's
Achievement of Order* (Baton Rouge, 1980), 153, xviii.

5. Michael Kreyling, *Author and Agent: Eudora Welty and Diarmuid Russell* (New
York, 1991), 108.

6. *Ibid.*

In *Sacred Groves and Ravaged Gardens: The Fiction of Eudora Welty, Carson McCullers, and Flannery O'Connor,* Louise Westling examines specifically the influence of Woolf's *To the Lighthouse* on Welty's expansion of "The Delta Cousins" into *Delta Wedding.* According to Westling, "As we explore the elements of *To the Lighthouse* which reappear in *Delta Wedding,* we . . . begin to see how only another woman could have helped Welty develop the celebration of distinctly feminine fertility and community which existed merely as germs in 'The Delta Cousins.' " [7] Westling's chapter perceptively illuminates similarities in the two novels' plots, characters, and themes. But I wish to argue that the relationship between these two novels does not depend as much on the fact that Woolf is a woman as it does on Woolf's interest in the novel as a field for consciously exploring gender constructions and the relationship between gender and genre.

Although Kreyling and Westling have provided the groundwork for a study of Woolf's influence upon Welty's development as a novelist, much remains to be said about this important literary relationship. This study explores the ways in which Welty incorporates and transforms in each of her major novels the concerns she inherited from Woolf and the ways in which this process helped Welty to define her own stance as an artist. Because Woolf is so central a figure in the development of the modern novel, this study locates Welty's fiction in the tradition of modernism. It examines Welty's interest in extending the boundaries of the novel as a genre and elements of her fiction that are sometimes neglected in an emphasis on local color or the southern grotesque, an emphasis to which Welty objects strongly. [8] The southern qualities of Welty's fiction, her participation in (and differences from) the techniques and concerns

7. Louise Westling, *Sacred Groves and Ravaged Gardens: The Fiction of Eudora Welty, Carson McCullers, and Flannery O'Connor* (Athens, Ga., 1985), 68.

8. Asked by Alice Walker in a 1973 interview, "Have you been called a Gothic Writer?" Welty responds energetically, "They better not call me that!" She continues, "Yes, I have been, though. Inevitably, because I'm a Southerner" (*C,* 137). See also Ruth Weston, *Gothic Traditions and Narrative Techniques in the Fiction of Eudora Welty* (Baton Rouge, 1994), 1–3. Weston persuasively demonstrates that Welty is rejecting an association with "the popular Gothic (upper case) genre of 'escape' fiction" rather than the tradition Weston traces back through Hawthorne, Byron, and others.

of other southern writers, have been the subject of much excellent critical attention.[9] Much less attention has been paid, however, to placing Welty's work in a context of writers and literary trends outside the South.[10] This study seeks to create a new context in which to read Welty's works.

The term *influence* does not necessarily imply that Welty's work is derivative of Woolf's or less than original and stamped with her own characteristic voice and vision. But a discussion of influence, of the ways that one writer makes use of his/her predecessors' works, is fraught with problems because, all too often, the term *influence* is read as synonymous with *imitation* and is used to slight an author's originality and creative powers. For instance, the question of James Joyce's influence on Woolf has been used by several critics to suggest that Woolf is not as significant an innovator as Joyce and is, somehow, a second- rather than first-rate artist.[11] John Crowe Ransom, after merely mentioning a resemblance to Woolf's work he believes to be fortuitous, is quick to defend Welty's "artistic integrity," as though his comment might be misconstrued as an insult to Welty's work: "Miss Welty's prose, like her people, is her own."[12]

9. See Rubin, *The Faraway Country*, 131–54; Louis D. Rubin, Jr., *A Gallery of Southerners* (Baton Rouge, 1982), 49–65; Albert J. Devlin, *Eudora Welty's Chronicle: A Story of Mississippi Life* (Jackson, 1983), *passim;* Carol S. Manning, *With Ears Opening Like Morning Glories: Eudora Welty and the Love of Storytelling* (Westport, Conn., 1985), *passim;* Westling, *Sacred Groves and Ravaged Gardens*, 65–109; Will Brantley, *Feminine Sense in Southern Memoir: Smith, Glasgow, Welty, Hellman, Porter, and Hurston* (Jackson, 1993), 36–132; Louise Westling, "Fathers and Daughters in Welty and O'Connor," in *The Female Tradition in Southern Literature*, ed. Carol S. Manning (Urbana, 1993), 110–24; Peggy Whitman Prenshaw, "Southern Ladies and the Southern Literary Renaissance," in *The Female Tradition*, ed. Manning, 73–88.

10. See Rubin, *A Gallery of Southerners*, 52; Peggy Whitman Prenshaw, "The Antiphonies of Eudora Welty's *One Writer's Beginnings* and Elizabeth Bowen's *Pictures and Conversations*," in *Welty: A Life in Literature*, ed. Albert J. Devlin (Jackson, 1987), 225–37; Chester E. Eisinger, "Traditionalism and Modernism in Eudora Welty," in *Eudora Welty: Critical Essays*, ed. Peggy Whitman Prenshaw (Jackson, 1979), 3–25; Jan Nordby Gretlund, "The Terrible and the Marvelous: Eudora Welty's Chekhov," in *Eudora Welty: The Eye of the Storyteller*, ed. Dawn Trouard (Kent, Ohio, 1989), 107–18.

11. Jean Guiguet, *Virginia Woolf and Her Works*, trans. Jean Stewart (New York, 1976), 241–47. Guiguet devotes six pages to defending Virginia Woolf against charges that her work is derivative of Joyce's and Proust's.

12. Ransom, "Delta Fiction," 504.

If Welty herself often reacts strongly to suggestions of influence, it is because the term does carry these suggestions of imitation, of inappropriate and inartistic reliance on the creativity of another. Like every contemporary southern novelist, Welty has been asked time and time again about Faulkner's influence upon her writing. While acknowledging that she learned from Faulkner "that a writer did not have to represent a dialect orthographically in order to create the sound of the dialect of a character's speech" (C, 280) and asserting that "his existence and his works mean a great deal to me" (C, 220), Welty resists the suggestion that her fiction is in any way indebted to his example: "Nobody can help you but yourself. So often I'm asked how I could have written a word with William Faulkner living in Mississippi, and this question amazes me. It was like living near a big mountain, something majestic—it made me happy to know it was there, all that work of his life. But it wasn't a helping or hindering presence. Its magnitude, all by itself, made it something remote in my own working life. When I thought of Faulkner was when I *read*" (C, 80). Elsewhere, discussing how she thinks literary influence operates, Welty says, "I think any influence would have to be indirect. . . . While I'm really in the process of working, I am not thinking about how anyone else does it or even how I ought to do it. . . . It would be a good thing if you could just go and influence yourself by the right person each time you find something wrong. But that's not the way it's done" (C, 19). Thus, while openly acknowledging Virginia Woolf's influence on her writing, Welty remains necessarily vague: "I know, even though I couldn't show in my work, heavens, the sense of what she has done certainly influenced me as an artist" (C, 325).

Certain theorists do, however, offer avenues of thinking about one writer's influence on another that illuminate the ways one text can incorporate others while avoiding the implication of direct imitation that Welty objects to in the term *influence*. Harold Bloom is one such theorist whose ideas, though widely recognized, are ill adapted for examining the influence of one woman writer on another. In *The Anxiety of Influence: A Theory of Poetry*, Bloom asserts that "poetic history . . . is held to be indistinguishable from poetic influence, since strong poets make that history by misreading one another, so as to clear imaginative space for themselves." Bloom's theory, which portrays literary influence as an Oedipal struggle between father and son, neglects women writers, and

his assumption of a fixed, shared literary tradition ignores the significance of gender in the construction of such a canon and in a writer's perception of and relation to such a tradition. But Welty's concept of "sweet devouring" and Woolf's claim, "For we think back through our mothers if we are women" (*ROO*, 79), suggest a markedly different model of influence for women. As Jane Marcus notes, "Woolf knew by experience how women influence each other. Far from Harold Bloom's concept of the 'anxiety of influence,' it is rather the opposite, affording the woman writer relief from anxiety." In "Reading Ourselves: Toward a Feminist Theory of Reading," Patrocinio P. Schweickart repositions the struggle for feminist writers and critics; she finds it in their relationship to the sort of patriarchal literary tradition that Bloom takes for granted: "Feminist critics may well say with Harold Bloom that reading always involves the 'art of defensive warfare.' What they mean by this, however, would not be Bloom's individualistic, agonistic encounter between 'strong poet' and 'strong reader,' but something more akin to 'class struggle.' Whether concerned with male or female texts, feminist criticism is situated in the larger struggle against patriarchy."[13]

Mikhail Bakhtin's theories of the novel and his concepts of dialogism and heteroglossia provide a more appropriate and useful way of perceiving and talking about relationships among works of literary art. As Bakhtin explains in *The Dialogic Imagination*, every writer is influenced, not only by the literary accomplishments of previous writers, but also by the various, conflicting ideologies and languages of his or her social and cultural milieu: "Language is not a neutral medium that passes freely and easily into the private property of the speaker's intentions; it is popu-

---

13. Harold Bloom, *The Anxiety of Influence: A Theory of Poetry* (Oxford, 1973), 5; Jane Marcus, "Thinking Back through Our Mothers," in *New Feminist Essays on Virginia Woolf*, ed. Jane Marcus (Lincoln, Nebr., 1981), 8; Patrocinio P. Schweickart, "Reading Ourselves: Toward A Feminist Theory of Reading," in *Feminisms: An Anthology of Literary Theory and Criticism*, ed. Robyn R. Warhol and Diane Price Herndl (New Brunswick, N.J., 1991), 542. See also Annette Kolodny, "A Map for Rereading: Gender and the Interpretation of Literary Texts," in *New Feminist Criticism: Essays on Women, Literature, and Theory*, ed. Elaine Showalter (New York, 1985), 46–62; Sandra M. Gilbert and Susan Gubar, *The Madwoman in the Attic: The Woman Writer and the Nineteenth-Century Imagination* (New Haven, 1979), 46–53.

lated—overpopulated—with the intentions of others. Expropriating it, forcing it to submit to one's own intentions and accents, is a difficult and complicated process." He argues that "the style of a novel is to be found in the combination of its styles; the language of a novel is the system of its 'languages.'" One way this expropriation of another's language takes place is through a dialogue among varying or conflicting styles, themes, ideologies: "The whole matter consists in the fact that there may be, between 'languages,' highly specific dialogic relations; no matter how these languages are conceived, they may all be taken as particular points of view on the world." [14]

One intention, one voice and language populating the form, structure, and thematic concerns of Welty's fiction is that of Virginia Woolf. Rather than a fixed, static object to be imitated, Woolf's fiction provides for Welty what Bakhtin calls an "internally persuasive discourse—as opposed to one that is externally authoritative," a discourse that is "half-ours and half-someone else's." This "internally persuasive discourse" acts as a creative, awakening force: "Its creativity and productiveness consist precisely in the fact that such a word *awakens new and independent words, that it organizes masses of our words from within, and does not remain in an isolated and static condition. It is not so much interpreted by us as it is further, that is, freely, developed, applied to new material, new conditions; it enters into interanimating relationships with new contexts.*" [15]

Bakhtin uses the concept of the "internally persuasive word" to theorize about "instances of powerful influence exercised by another's discourse on a given author." He explains that "when such influences are laid bare, the half-concealed life lived by another's discourse is revealed within the new context of the given author. *When such an influence is deep and productive, there is no external imitation, no simple act of reproduction, but rather a further creative development of another's (more precisely, half-other) discourse in a new context and under new conditions.*" Thus, through this dialogic engagement with another's discourse, the author develops his/her voice(s) and discourse(s): "The importance of struggling with another's

14. Mikhail M. Bakhtin, *The Dialogic Imagination: Four Essays,* ed. Michael Holquist, trans. Caryl Emerson and Michael Holquist (Austin, 1981), 294, 262, 293.
15. *Ibid.,* 345–46 (emphasis added).

discourse, its influence in the history of an individual's coming to ideo-
logical consciousness, is enormous. One's own discourse and one's own
voice, although born of another or dynamically stimulated by another,
will sooner or later begin to liberate themselves from the authority of
the other's discourse." [16]

The dynamic that Bakhtin describes in these passages is similar to the
feminist paradigm of reading that Schweickart outlines. Schweickart describes the relationship between the feminist reader and the woman
writer as "dialogic." She argues that although "in all stories of reading,
the drama revolves around the subject-object relationship between text
and reader," in the feminist "story of reading" this relationship is "an
intersubjective construction. . . . The reader encounters not simply a
text, but . . . comes into close contact with an interiority—a power, a
creativity, a suffering, a vision—that is *not* identical with her own."
Schweickart, however, offers an alternative to the Bakhtinian notion of
struggle and his use of battle metaphors to describe the relationship between the author and the "internally persuasive voice." In Schweickart's
description of "the dialectic of communication informing the relationship between the feminist reader and the female author/text, the central
issue is not of control or partition, but of managing the contradictory
implications of the desire for relationship (one must maintain a minimal
distance from the other) and the desire for intimacy, up to and including
a symbiotic merger with the other." [17]

Seen in light of Bakhtin's and Schweickart's ideas, Welty's creative
engagement and imaginative dialogue with Woolf's fiction becomes one
of the forces leading to Welty's development as a novelist. Examining and
reconsidering Woolf's (re)conception of the novel's form and exploration
of gender issues, Welty has defined her creative language and vision.
Exploring Welty's appropriation of and response to Woolf's fiction within
the context of these theoretical perspectives allows us to study Welty's
development as a writer and brings to our attention features of her work
obscured by her categorization as a southern writer. Reading these two

16. *Ibid.*, 347 (emphasis added), 348.
17. Schweickart, "Reading Ourselves," 542, 544.

writers in tandem provides as well a new context or perspective from which to consider Woolf's artistic achievement.

One important dialogue between Virginia Woolf's and Eudora Welty's novels concerns the portrayal of women. That Woolf considered herself a feminist and was concerned with women's issues, especially with problems confronting women artists, is obvious from her essays and novels, and her fiction has been the focus of much feminist criticism.[18] Numerous readers have described Welty's work as also being somehow "feminine." Ransom says of *Delta Wedding,* "It is needless to remark that this is a woman's book." J. A. Bryant, Jr., describes Welty's narrative voice in *Losing Battles* as "pretty surely female."[19]

Welty's preference for female protagonists and narrators, and her attention to traditionally female activities, roles, and ceremonies—mothering, cooking, housekeeping, weddings, reunions—prompted critics in the 1970s to begin viewing her work from feminist perspectives. For example, Elizabeth M. Kerr compares the initiation rituals of Welty's young women to those of Faulkner's young men. Margaret Jones Bosterli argues that Welty's "novels are about the women's culture" and that "the interactions of these women, their relationship with each other, and their visions of life . . . form the fabric of the novels." Peggy Whitman Prenshaw extends this argument, examining what she sees as the matriarchal order of Welty's fiction.[20]

18. See Carolyn Heilbrun, *Toward a Recognition of Androgyny* (New York, 1973), 151–67; all of the essays in Marcus, ed., *New Feminist Essays;* Toril Moi, *Sexual/Textual Politics* (New York, 1985), 1–18; Rachel Blau DuPlessis, *Writing Beyond the Ending: Narrative Strategies of Twentieth-Century Women Writers* (Bloomington, Ind., 1985), 162–77; Elizabeth A. Meese, *Crossing the Double Cross: The Practice of Feminist Criticism* (Chapel Hill, 1986), 89–114; Jane Marcus, *Virginia Woolf and the Languages of Patriarchy* (Bloomington, 1987); Elizabeth Abel, *Virginia Woolf and the Fictions of Psychoanalysis* (Chicago, 1989), 1–29; Pamela L. Caughie, *Virginia Woolf and Postmodernism* (Urbana, 1991), 1–27; Elizabeth Abel, "Narrative Structure(s) and Female Development," in *Virginia Woolf: A Collection of Critical Essays,* ed. Margaret Homans (Englewood Cliffs, N.J., 1993), 93–114; Marianne Hirsch, "The Darkest Plots: Narration and Compulsory Heterosexuality," in *Virginia Woolf,* ed. Homans, 196–209.

19. Ransom, "Delta Fiction," 504; J. A. Bryant, Jr., "The Recovery of the Confident Narrator: *A Curtain of Green* to *Losing Battles,*" in *Critical Essays,* ed. Prenshaw, 77.

20. Elizabeth M. Kerr, "The World of Eudora Welty's Women," in *Critical Essays,*

During the 1980s and 1990s, feminist criticism of Welty's fiction became even more popular and more theoretical. Patricia Yaeger combines Bakhtin's theories of the novel with the critical thought of French feminists Hélène Cixous and Luce Irigaray to examine Welty's incorporation and revision of W. B. Yeats's poetry in *The Golden Apples*. Elizabeth Evans' "Eudora Welty and the Dutiful Daughter" examines the complex relationships between mothers and daughters in *The Optimist's Daughter* and *The Golden Apples;* Marilyn Arnold offers a feminist rereading of *The Ponder Heart*. Franziska Gygax's book-length study, *Serious Daring from Within: Female Narrative Strategies in Eudora Welty's Novels,* draws upon a combination of feminist theories and narratology to explore Welty's narrative strategies. Peter Schmidt's *The Heart of the Story: Eudora Welty's Short Fiction* analyzes the influence of nineteenth-century American women writers on Welty's fiction. Ann Romines devotes two chapters to Welty's fiction in her study of domestic ritual in American fiction. In his study of southern women's autobiographies, Will Brantley links Welty's *One Writer's Beginnings* with Ellen Glasgow's *The Woman Within,* arguing that both writers demonstrate "that a sheltered existence need not stifle one's sense of self." In *The Female Tradition in Southern Literature,* Peggy Whitman Prenshaw's essay considers Welty in the context of the southern literary renaissance, while Louise Westling's essay on fathers and daughters contrasts "Welty's comic vision of daughters and their fathers" to Flannery O'Connor's "tragic one." Gail Mortimer's *Daughter of the Swan: Love and Knowledge in Eudora Welty's Fiction* uses feminist psychological theories to illuminate patterns of autonomy and connection in Welty's work. In *The Dragon's Blood: Feminist Intertextuality in Eudora Welty's "The Golden Apples,"* Rebecca Mark demonstrates Welty's critique and revision of the Western heroic literary tradition in *The Golden Apples*.[21]

---

ed. Prenshaw, 132–48; Margaret Jones Bosterli, "Woman's Vision: The Worlds of Women in *Delta Wedding, Losing Battles* and *The Optimist's Daughter,*" in *Critical Essays,* ed. Prenshaw, 149; Peggy Whitman Prenshaw, "Woman's World, Man's Place: The Fiction of Eudora Welty," in *Eudora Welty: A Form of Thanks,* ed. Louis Dollarhide and Ann J. Abadie (Jackson, 1979), 46–77.

21. Patricia Yaeger, "Because a Fire Was in My Head: Eudora Welty and the Dialogic Imagination," in *Welty,* ed. Devlin, 136–67; Elizabeth Evans, "Eudora Welty and

Despite this wealth of feminist criticism of her works, Welty often resists being labeled a "woman writer" in the same way she resists being categorized as a southern or gothic writer. In most of her comments about feminism, Welty defines it as a political movement rather than a theoretical construct or an epistemology. Welty articulates her reasons for disliking any association of her art with political causes in "Must the Novelist Crusade?" In this essay she argues that a political agenda interferes with the quality of a writer's imaginative work: "Passion is the chief ingredient of good fiction. . . . But to distort a work of passion for the sake of a cause is to cheat, and the end, far from justifying the means, is fairly sure to be lost with it" (E, 156–57). When asked by Charles T. Bunting in a 1972 interview, "Why have there been so few really great women writers?" Welty replies at length:

> I am a woman. In writing fiction, I think imagination comes ahead of sex. . . . Well, I think there have been not a few great women writers, of course. Jane Austen. I don't see how anyone could have a greater scope in knowledge of human nature and reveal more of human nature than Jane Austen. Consider Virginia Woolf. The Brontës. Well, you know as many as I do: great women writers. I'm not interested in any kind of a feminine repartee. I don't care what sex people are when they write. I just want the result to be a good book. All that talk of women's lib doesn't apply *at all* to women writers. We've always been able to do what we've wished. I couldn't feel less deprived as a woman to be writing, and I certainly enjoy all the feelings of any other

the Dutiful Daughter," in *Eye of the Storyteller,* ed. Trouard, 57–68; Marilyn Arnold, "The Strategy of Edna Earle Ponder," in *Eye of the Storyteller,* ed. Trouard, 69–77; Franziska Gygax, *Serious Daring from Within: Female Narrative Strategies in Eudora Welty's Novels* (Westport, Conn., 1990), *passim;* Peter Schmidt, *The Heart of the Story: Eudora Welty's Short Fiction* (Jackson, 1991), 204–65; Ann Romines, *The Home Plot: Women, Writing and Domestic Ritual* (Amherst, 1992), 192–291; Brantley, *Feminine Sense in Southern Memoir,* 87; Peggy Whitman Prenshaw, "Southern Ladies and the Southern Literary Renaissance," in *The Female Tradition,* ed. Manning, 73–88; Louise Westling, "Fathers and Daughters in Welty and O'Connor," in *The Female Tradition,* ed. Manning, 111; Gail Mortimer, *Daughter of the Swan: Love and Knowledge in Eudora Welty's Fiction* (Athens, Ga., 1994); Rebecca Mark, *The Dragon's Blood: Feminist Interextuality in Eudora Welty's "The Golden Apples"* (Jackson, 1994).

human being. The full complement is available. I have the point of view of a woman, but if I'm not able to imagine myself into what another human being who is a man might feel, which I have to do all the time when I write, well, it's just from poverty of imagination. It's a matter of imagination, not sex. (*C,* 54)

Louise Westling comments perceptively on the ambivalence of Welty's answer to this question: "First, in response to the questioner's condescension, Welty defends the achievements of women writers; then she backs away, dissociating herself from feminism. Yet all the writers she mentions are distinctively feminine in their treatment of theme, point of view, and setting." [22]

Virginia Woolf is actually no less ambivalent than Welty on the question of the relationship of sex to writing. The following passage from the concluding pages of *A Room of One's Own,* Woolf's extended essay devoted to the topic "Women and Fiction," expresses a similar attitude: "Even so, the very first sentence that I would write here, I said, crossing over to the writing-table and taking up the page headed Women and Fiction, is that it is fatal for anyone who writes to think of their sex. It is fatal to be a man or woman pure and simple. One must be woman-manly or man-womanly" (*ROO,* 108).

At the heart of Woolf's and Welty's ambivalence lies a debate that has been central to discussions of women's writing from before Woolf's time to the present: When we talk about "women's writing" and "men's writing," are we referring to biological or sociocultural differences? Both writers reject an essentialist stance, the suggestion that the way they write is biologically determined and limited by their sex. Certainly, recent literary theory suggests that biological definitions do not help us much in discussions of women's writing. It is more useful (but no less problematic) in a study that examines the works of two women writers, one English and one American, to consider questions of women's (or feminine or feminist) writing in the context of English and American literary and philosophical traditions, in the context of Western discourse. This discourse is dominated, argues Shoshana Felman, by "the metaphysical

22. Westling, *Sacred Groves and Ravaged Gardens,* 67.

logic of dichotomous oppositions . . . (Presence/Absence, Being/Noth-ingness, Truth/Error, Same/Other, Identity/Difference, etc.)." Man/ Woman and Masculine/Feminine follow in this pattern of opposition. The terms of each dichotomy are not equal; instead, they form a hier-archy in which *man* and *self* are primary and *woman* and *other* are sec-ondary and dependent. Woman, claims Simone de Beauvoir, "is defined and differentiated with reference to man, and not he with reference to her; she is the incidental, the inessential as opposed to the essential. He is the subject, he is the Absolute—she is the Other."[23]

To define woman solely in terms of her relationship to and difference from man is to define woman not just as other, but as absence, negation, and lack, and as silent, excluded from language. But, as Diane Price Herndl asks, "When woman is in a position analogous to Silence, Ab-sence, and Madness in the paradigm of Western thought (Speech/Silence, Presence/Absence, Logic/Madness) . . . what happens to her language?" Or, in Felman's words, "How can the woman be thought about outside of the Masculine/Feminine framework, other than as opposed to man, without being subordinated to a primordial masculine mold? . . . How can difference as such be thought out as non-subordinate to identity? In other words, how can thought [and writing] break away from the logic of polar opposites?"[24]

Toril Moi argues that removing identity from this traditional gender hierarchy is one of the primary features and goals of Woolf's fiction and nonfiction. Moi claims that Woolf rejects traditional gender identities "because she has seen them for what they are. She has understood that the goal of the feminist struggle must precisely be to deconstruct the death-dealing binary oppositions of masculinity and femininity."[25] I wish to argue that Welty's fiction shares this passion, seeking radically new character and textual identities that are neither repressive nor limiting.

23. Shoshana Felman, "Woman and Madness: The Critical Phallacy," *Diacritics,* V (Winter, 1975), 7; Simone de Beauvoir, *The Second Sex,* trans. and ed. H. M. Parshley (1953; rpr. New York, 1974), xvi.

24. Diane Price Herndl, "The Dilemmas of a Feminine Dialogic," in *Feminism, Bakhtin, and the Dialogic,* ed. Dale M. Bauer and Susan Jaret McKinstry (Albany, 1991), 10; Felman, "Woman and Madness," 4.

25. Moi, *Sexual/Textual Politics,* 13.

Both writers use the novel as a ground for exploring alternatives to the rigid and limiting dualism of the binary oppositions.

Mary Jacobus explains that when female difference is removed from this hierarchical opposition, when Otherness is defined as multiplicity rather than lack, the result in terms of feminist criticism is significant: "*Difference* is redefined, not as male *versus* female—not as biologically constituted—but as a multiplicity, ambiguity and heterogeneity which is that of textuality itself. Writing, the production of meaning, becomes the site both of challenge and otherness; rather than (as in more traditional approaches) simply yielding the themes and representation of female oppression."[26] When the duality of the monologic, authoritarian hierarchy is replaced by a dialogic multiplicity, the feminine stance becomes one of freedom, creativity, and power instead of remaining a position of powerlessness and dependency. Virginia Woolf's fiction provided Welty with a model of just this sort of feminist narrative practice.

Here again, Bakhtin's theories are useful to this study. The novel, he claims, is the genre most suited to this multiplicity because its inherent dialogism resists these traditional hierarchies and oppositions. In his preface to *Bakhtin: Essays and Dialogues on His Work*, Gary Saul Morson argues that "perhaps Bakhtin's most radical contribution lies in his rethinking of traditional oppositions: of the individual to society, of self to other, of the specific utterance to the totality of language, and of particular actions to the world of norms and conventions."[27] As, in Bakhtin's terms, "the only developing genre," existing in "a living contact with unfinished, still-evolving contemporary reality (the openended present)," the novel becomes the site for *heteroglossia*—language's conflicting, interacting voices—the voices of narrators, characters, other genres, social structures, and ideologies.[28]

26. Mary Jacobus, *Reading Women: Essays in Feminist Criticism* (New York, 1986), 30.

27. Gary Saul Morson, "Preface: Perhaps Bakhtin," in *Bakhtin: Essays and Dialogues on His Work,* ed. Gary Saul Morson (Chicago, 1986), xi.

28. Bakhtin, *The Dialogic Imagination,* 4, 7. Bakhtin's comments about the novel's close contact with contemporary reality are similar to Welty's ideas about the novel that she explains in her essay "Place in Fiction." The novel, says Welty, is the genre that "speaks [the truth] most unmistakably, most directly, most variously, most fully. . . . Why?

Though Bakhtin employs language and concepts similar to those used by many feminist critics, he ignores the issue of gender in his discussions of the novel. However, critics such as Wayne C. Booth, Diane Price Herndl, Dale M. Bauer, and Patricia Yaeger have examined the intersection of Bakhtin's ideas with issues raised by feminist theory. In "Freedom of Interpretation: Bakhtin and the Challenge of Feminist Criticism," Booth asks, "Is it not remarkable to discover no hint in such a penetrating and exhaustive inquiry into how our various dialects are constituted, no shadow of a suggestion in the lists and the 'and so forths' of the influence of sexual differences, no hint that women now talk or have ever talked in ways different from men's? . . . The omission is so glaring that it makes one long for the skill to make up for it." [29]

Current theorists are attempting to make up for this omission. For example, Price Herndl explains that "like Bakhtin's theory of novelistic discourse, theories of feminine language describe a multivoiced or polyphonic resistance to hierarchies and laughter at authority. Furthermore, in the hierarchies Bakhtin mentions, the novel always takes the woman's structural place as the excluded other: masculine/feminine, epic/novel, poetry/novel." Dale M. Bauer defines a "feminist dialogics [as] a paradigm which acknowledges individual acts of reading as an experience of otherness and challenges the cultural powers which often force us to contain or restrict the otherness of textual voices." She asserts that "for feminists, Bakhtin's theories of the social nature of the utterance—both the inner and outer words—provide a critical language that allows us to pinpoint and foreground the moments when the patriarchal work and the persuasive resistance to it come into conflict. By highlighting these contradictions, a feminist dialogics produces occasions for the disruption and critique of dominant and oppressive ideologies." Patricia Yaeger's combination of Bakhtin's theories and feminist theories in "Because a Fire Was in My Head" provides an early illustration of the value of a

---

Because the novel from the start has been bound up in the local, the 'real,' the present, the ordinary day-to-day of human experience. . . . Fiction is properly at work on the here and now, or the past made here and now; for in the novels we have to be there" (E, 117).

29. Wayne C. Booth, "Freedom of Interpretation: Bakhtin and the Challenge of Feminist Criticism," *Critical Inquiry*, IX (1982), 60.

feminist Bakhtinian perspective in reading Welty's fiction. Yaeger concludes that although Bakhtin does not address gender issues in his own work, his "theories of linguistic evolution, of dialogism, and of heteroglossia will give us a useful vocabulary and a new perspective from which to examine the central tensions between men's and women's writing."[30]

In their experiments with narrative voice and structure, Virginia Woolf and Eudora Welty create such a feminist dialogics, exploiting the heteroglossia inherent in language, decentering the authority of the narrator or author, and giving full play to the novel's many voices. Their works gain energy from the multiplicity of their many-voiced narrative structures. In novels such as *Mrs. Dalloway* (1925), *To the Lighthouse* (1927), *The Waves* (1931), *Delta Wedding* (1946), and *Losing Battles* (1970), narrative perspective and voice are distributed among characters with varied and distinctive views. In fact, the difference among these characters' varying orientations to reality becomes one subject these novels examine. *Orlando* (1928), *Between the Acts* (1941), *The Robber Bridegroom* (1942), *The Golden Apples* (1949), and *The Optimist's Daughter* (1972) add to the dialogue among characters and narrators an intertextual dialogue among varying genres.

Woolf and Welty incorporate different genres into the context of their novels and thus feminize or novelize them. Such feminization/novelization explores and calls into question the underlying assumptions of the genres. The dialogue created by Welty's reconsideration of Woolf's narrative techniques, structures, and thematic concerns illustrates the ways in which Woolf's fiction modeled for Welty the varied strategies a writer can use to appropriate, transgress, and transform patriarchal discourse.

Each chapter of this study examines a pair of novels, one by Virginia Woolf and one by Eudora Welty. In addition to exploring the dialogue between the works and the ways in which Welty's fiction is marked by her "devouring" of Woolf's works, each chapter also illustrates one of the strategies these two women writers use as they seek to appropriate

30. Price Herndl, "The Dilemmas of a Feminine Dialogic," in *Feminism, Bakhtin, and the Dialogic,* ed. Bauer and McKinstry, 8; Dale M. Bauer, *Feminist Dialogics: A Theory of Failed Community* (Albany, 1988), 673; Dale M. Bauer, "Introduction," in *Feminism, Bakhtin, and the Dialogic,* ed. Bauer and McKinstry, 3; Yaeger, "Because a Fire Was in My Head," in *Welty,* ed. Devlin, 142.

traditional masculine narrative forms and languages. As Bakhtin says, "This process—experimenting by turning persuasive discourse into speaking persons—becomes especially important in those cases where a struggle against such images has already begun, where someone is striving to liberate himself [in this case, herself] from the influence of such an image and its discourse by means of objectification, or is striving to expose the limitations of both image and discourse." [31] In *To the Lighthouse* Woolf uses this strategy to dramatize the tension between traditional gender roles in romance through the interplay of attraction and antagonism between Mr. and Mrs. Ramsay. At the same time, other characters voice various cultural perspectives on gender and romance. As these views interrogate one another, the "naturalness" of traditional gender roles is called into question. In the same way, *Delta Wedding* questions gender-based familial roles as well as romantic roles. By using the novel as a site for the expression of women's views—oftentimes marginalized and silenced in the patriarchal plantation society represented in the novel— Welty draws the southern patriarchal constructs of family and society into dialogue with alternative views.

Intertextuality is another strategy that women writers use to appropriate and revise cultural narratives that seek to marginalize and silence women. Woolf and Welty incorporate a variety of different genres— pastoral, history, biography, fairy tale, epic, and elegy—into their works as well as make intertextual use of specific texts. In novelizing or feminizing these various genres, making them part of each work's internal dialogue, Woolf and Welty question the different genres' cultural assumptions, assumptions that often have a masculine bias. As Rachel Blau DuPlessis argues, "Narrative structures and subjects are like working apparatuses of ideology, factories for the 'natural' and 'fantastic' meanings by which we live. Here are produced and disseminated the assumptions, the conflicts, the patterns that create fictional boundaries for experience. . . . To compose a work is to negotiate with these questions: What stories can be told? How can plots be resolved? What is felt to be narratable by both literary and social standards?" [32]

---

31. Bakhtin, *The Dialogic Imagination,* 348.
32. DuPlessis, *Writing Beyond the Ending,* 3; see also Mark, *The Dragon's Blood,* 3–30.

Intertextuality provides Woolf and Welty with a way of appropriating "masculine" genres and raising questions about the ideologies implicit in those forms. Thus speculation about the questions DuPlessis asks becomes a subtext of the novels in this study. *Orlando* poses questions about the purposes of biography and explores the assumptions that have determined the types of behavior deemed appropriate to biographical writing. *The Robber Bridegroom* poses similar questions about historical discourse and the assumptions encoded in traditional historical narrative forms. Thus Woolf and Welty use the novel's multivoiced form to examine the construction of cultural narratives in two exuberantly comic novels that transgress boundaries and challenge expectations at every turn. Central to *The Waves* and *Losing Battles* is a struggle between an idealized, final epic past and the open-ended, incomplete present of the novel. Participating in this struggle, a communal chorus battles against the emergence of individual voices seeking self-definition. Both novels use a circular and multivoiced narrative to undermine the authority of a central, unified narrator. In the works throughout this study Woolf and Welty use the novel as a ground for exploring alternative narrative forms.

Constructing new images of female artists and seeking to redefine and revalue art outside of a phallocentric paradigm is the final strategy this study explores in the works of Woolf and Welty. Woolf has created a variety of female artists: Lily Briscoe is a painter; Orlando is a writer; and Mrs. Ramsay is an artist of social situations and domestic settings. All struggle to reconcile their artistic impulses with their social roles as women. In Welty's fiction, we see a progression in the development of female artists. The women of *The Robber Bridegroom* use lies and plotting—consciously constructed narratives—as a means of artistically manipulating and gaining control of their lives. *Delta Wedding*'s Laura McRaven shows promise of both artistic ability and the determination to pattern her own life. *Losing Battles* offers a more positive portrait of women and art, as the Beecham and Renfro women pattern the family's life through their continuous storytelling. Finally, in *The Optimist's Daughter,* Welty creates a protagonist who is an artist by vocation as well as avocation. Laurel McKelva Hand's medium is graphic design, and she works to discover and fulfill the patterns in her life. For Welty, as for Woolf, the successful woman artist is one who can bring her vision to

bear upon her life as well as her art. Being an artist, in the fiction of these two writers, involves more than producing works of art. To be an artist is to engage in a process of patterning and of situating oneself in relation to others.

I

QUALIFIED PASTORALS
Delta Wedding and *To the Lighthouse*

I N "Discourse in the Novel," Bakhtin asks the reader to think of the novel not as "a self-sufficient and closed authorial monologue, one that presumes only passive listeners beyond its own boundaries," but as "a rejoinder in a given dialogue, whose style is determined by its interrelationship with other rejoinders in the same dialogue (in the totality of the conversation)." Virginia Woolf's letters, essays, and diaries reveal that she saw her own writing as part of many ongoing dialogues, particularly about the novel itself, its structure, its possibilities as a genre, and its capacity for expressing women's realities. Eudora Welty entered into a dialogue with Woolf upon first reading *To the Lighthouse,* which, she says in her foreword to that novel, "opened the door of imaginative fiction for me." [1] In *Delta Wedding,* Welty made this dialogue central to her first attempt at writing a full-length novel. Set in a country house full of children and visitors, and presided over by a strong and attractive mother figure, *Delta Wedding* reconsiders and responds to many of Woolf's major concerns in *To the Lighthouse,* such as the decentering of narrative authority and point of view, the use and critique of a pastoral setting and world view, and the construction of feminine identity and subjectivity.

Although Louise Westling's discussion of *Delta Wedding* in *Sacred Groves and Ravaged Gardens* focuses primarily upon the novel's extensive

1. Bakhtin, *The Dialogic Imagination,* 274; Welty, Foreword to *To the Lighthouse,* vii.

mythological reverberations, examining in particular Welty's use of the Demeter and Kore myth, Westling also addresses the importance of *To the Lighthouse* to Welty's writing of her first full novel. Westling argues that *To the Lighthouse*, "Virginia Woolf's dramatization of family life centered on a mother's creative power," provided a prototype for *Delta Wedding*, which she calls a "pastoral hymn of fertility." She notes many of the similarities in plot, setting, and motif of *Delta Wedding* and *To the Lighthouse* "appropriate . . . for the celebration of family life and fertility." Both are set in September "under a harvest moon, in a family sanctuary removed from the distractions of public life." Westling describes Ellen Fairchild as "a mother figure equal in sensitivity to Woolf's Mrs. Ramsay" and points out that both Mrs. Ramsay and Ellen Fairchild are concerned with marriage and engage in matchmaking. Westling discusses some specific "echoes" of *To the Lighthouse* that show up in *Delta Wedding*— "scenes of motherly care for children," the lost pin motif, and bees. She observes as well that Battle Fairchild, like Mr. Ramsay, often comments upon life by reciting poetry.[2] One amusing similarity Westling doesn't mention is Welty's repetition of the refrain, "Damn your eyes," the song Nancy, Andrew, Paul, and Minta sing in *To the Lighthouse* as they walk along the cliff by the sea (*TL,* 113). In *Delta Wedding,* Roy, one of the Fairchild children, sings, "My name is Samuel Hall and I hate you one and all, damn your eyes!" (*DW,* 126). In addition, Mrs. Ramsay's description of her essential self as "a wedge-shaped core of darkness" (*TL,* 95) is echoed in India Fairchild's description of Troy Flavin as "a black wedge in the lighted window" (*DW,* 53).

Westling argues that by "taking up Virginia Woolf's themes of marriage and the maternal role from *To the Lighthouse,* Eudora Welty was unconsciously agreeing with that novel's argument for the central power of womanhood." *Delta Wedding* does indeed take up the concerns of motherhood and marriage, among others, from *To the Lighthouse,* but I believe the relationship between the two novels goes beyond an unconscious agreement on Welty's part with Woolf's treatment of these issues.

2. Westling, *Sacred Groves and Ravaged Gardens,* 65–71; Gygax, *Serious Daring from Within,* 35, also identifies similarities between Mrs. Ramsay and Ellen Fairchild: "They are mothers, troubled by their daily commitments, yet intensely susceptible to the meaning of a moment, of beauty."

(In fact, Woolf's own attitude toward issues of feminine or maternal power is shifting and ambivalent throughout *To the Lighthouse.*) *Delta Wedding* does not merely mirror, imitate, or agree with, but responds to *To the Lighthouse.* The relationship between the two novels is a complex example of Bakhtin's "active engaged understanding," which "assimilates the word to be understood into its own conceptual system filled with specific objects and emotional expressions, and is indissolubly merged with the response, with a *motivated agreement or disagreement.* To some extent, primacy belongs to the response, as the activating principle: it creates the ground for understanding, it prepares the ground for an active and engaged understanding. *Understanding comes to fruition only in the response.*" [3]

Delta Wedding is Welty's first response to *To the Lighthouse,* and the disagreements or divergences between these two novels tell us as much as the similarities do about Welty's development as a novelist. Welty adopts the many-voiced narrative structure of *To the Lighthouse* to explore and question many of the same gender issues, especially those having to do with masculine and feminine identities, but her exploration and her discoveries often lead her in directions different from Woolf's. Woolf's use of pastoral elements in *To the Lighthouse* is another narrative strategy Welty works with in *Delta Wedding.* But this early response to Woolf's *To the Lighthouse* sidesteps some of the darker implications of the "Time Passes" section and therefore does not achieve the ecstatic vision of the "Lighthouse" section. Still, Welty's novel raises many of the concerns that she treats more fully in her later novels, concerns that she encountered as a reader of *To the Lighthouse.*

THE PASTORAL PERSPECTIVE

The most obvious similarities between *Delta Wedding* and *To the Lighthouse* are with the "Window" section of Woolf's novel. Welty's Shellmound and Woolf's vacation house in the Hebrides are both full of life, echoing with the sounds of children and their activities. Both houses

3. Westling, *Sacred Groves and Ravaged Gardens,* 68; Bakhtin, *The Dialogic Imagination,* 282 (emphasis added).

show the wear and tear of such life in their shabbiness and disrepair. The families are similar as well. The Ramsays have seven children, the Fair-childs, eight; in each family the children vary in age from early childhood to late adolescence. In addition to the numerous family members, out-siders to the family are visiting in each novel. Some of these outsiders, like Lily Briscoe and Laura McRaven, are welcomed by the family; oth-ers, like Charles Tansley and Troy Flavin, are viewed with resentment as threats to the family's unity and happiness. In each novel the family with its satellites forms an insular, self-sufficient universe whose energies are directed toward perpetuating familial mythologies of unity and happiness and repressing any threats to or disruptions of the patriarchal order.

Seventeen-year-old Dabney Fairchild's approaching wedding creates a vacation-like air in the Fairchild family home and allows Welty to place an exploration of marital relationships at the center of her novel. Paul and Minta's engagement provides the impetus for similar explorations in *To the Lighthouse,* as do Lily Briscoe's unmarried status and Mrs. Ramsay's desire to change it. Although no one indulges in any matchmaking with Primrose and Jim Allen, the two unmarried aunts in *Delta Wedding,* they provide a similar counterpoint to the role of wife and mother typified by Ellen Fairchild. Meanwhile, Shelley Fairchild, Dabney's older sister, experiences guilt and rebellion, similar to Lily's, in the face of her younger sister's marriage.

The resemblance between Mrs. Ramsay and Ellen Fairchild noted by Westling and Vande Kieft has much to do with their primary roles as wives and mothers: they contemplate their children's personalities, fear for their children's futures, sing their children to sleep, measure their children for clothing, care for and protect their husbands and the other men in their households. They care, as well, for those outside the family; each woman makes a trip into the nearest town to look after an ailing neighbor, extending the boundaries of her maternal realm.

For both women, preparing food and providing meals for the family becomes synonymous with sustaining family connections and creating hope and love within the family. Mrs. Ramsay's dinner of *boeuf en daube* becomes a celebration of Paul and Minta's engagement, of marriage in general, and a triumph of the forces that unite humans over those that separate them:

Everything seemed possible. Everything seemed right. Just now . . . she had
reached security; she hovered like a hawk suspended; like a flag floated in
an element of joy which filled every nerve of her body fully and sweetly, not
noisily, solemnly rather, for it arose, she thought, looking at them all eating
there, from husband and children and friends; all of which rising in this
profound silence (she was helping William Bankes to one very small piece
more, and peered into the depths of the earthenware pot) seemed now for
no special reason to stay there like a smoke, like a fume rising upwards,
holding them safe together. Nothing need be said; nothing could be said.
There it was, all around them. It partook, she felt, carefully helping Mr.
Bankes to a specially tender piece, of eternity. (*TL,* 157–58)[4]

In a similar scene, Ellen Fairchild's cake baking merges with her concerns over her daughter's approaching marriage and her consideration of
George and Robbie Fairchild's marriage, until the success of the cake
and the success of these marriages become one and the same:

As Ellen put in the nutmeg and the grated lemon rind she diligently assumed
George's happiness, seeing it in the Fairchild aspects of exuberance and sa-
tiety; if it was unabashed, it was the best part true. But—adding the milk,
the egg whites, the flour, carefully and alternately as Mashula's recipe said—
she could be diligent and still not wholly sure—never wholly. She loved
George too dearly herself to seek her knowledge of him through the family
attitude, keen and subtle as that was—just as she loved Dabney too much
to see her prospect without its risk . . . the happiness covered with danger.
(*DW,* 26)

The nostalgia that pervades *Delta Wedding* and the "Window" section
of *To the Lighthouse* results from the pastoral elements in each: the sense
of seclusion and removal from the rest of the world, as London and
Memphis seem worlds away; the security, permanence, and renewal of
each setting; and the sheer beauty and delight in the natural settings, the

---

4. See also Louise Westling, "Food, Landscape and the Feminine in *Delta Wedding,*"
Southern Quarterly, XXX (1992), 29–30.

gardens, of each.[5] Maria DiBattista ties the pastoral tone of the first section of *To the Lighthouse* to Mrs. Ramsay: "As a type of the Great and Good Mother who contains and preserves the beauty of the world in a 'circle of life,' Mrs. Ramsay inspires the novel's pastoral imagery, an imagery emanating from a 'naive' vision of a beneficent, prolific, and artful Nature." John Edward Hardy calls *Delta Wedding* a "*conscious* exploring of the implications of the [pastoral] mode."[6]

But neither *To the Lighthouse* nor *Delta Wedding* can be accurately represented as a pure celebration of the nurturing, maternal, natural cycles of life. Neither Virginia Woolf nor Eudora Welty has written a naïvely pure "pastoral" novel. The pastoral qualities form one of the "languages" of *To the Lighthouse* and *Delta Wedding,* and provide Woolf and Welty one way of "incorporating and organizing heteroglossia" as they set up a dialogue between the pastoral and nonpastoral elements in their works.[7] At the same time that they celebrate the pastoral, the novels imply a criticism of the world view, of the ideology implicit in the pastoral genre.

This critique of the pastoral world view pervades *To the Lighthouse* and provides one of the primary sources of tension in the novel. Below the calm, harmonious surface of "The Window," we see a child's disappointment and anger at a tyrannical father, Mr. Ramsay's insecurities and feelings of failure, and Mrs. Ramsay's worries over the cost of greenhouse repairs. More important, direct criticism of the pastoral lies at the structural heart of the novel. Following Mrs. Ramsay's triumphant dinner that unifies the disparate beings around the table, creating order out of

5. Woolf's novel is not the only pastoral source behind Welty's *Delta Wedding,* as even a brief survey of the history of southern literature will demonstrate. See Lewis P. Simpson, *The Dispossessed Garden: Pastoral and History in Southern Literature* (Athens, Ga., 1975), 2; Jan Bakker, *Pastoral in Antebellum Southern Romance* (Baton Rouge, 1989), 1–3; Elizabeth Jane Harrison, *Female Pastoral: Women Writers Re-Visioning the American South* (Knoxville, 1991), 9–11; Albert J. Devlin, "Meeting the World in *Delta Wedding,*" in *Critical Essays on Eudora Welty,* ed. W. Craig Turner and Lee Emling Harding (Boston, 1989), 92.

6. Maria DiBattista, *Virginia Woolf's Major Novels: The Fables of Anon* (New Haven, 1980), 75; John Edward Hardy, "*Delta Wedding* as Region and Symbol," *Sewanee Review,* LX (1952), 400.

7. Bakhtin, *The Dialogic Imagination,* 320.

chaos and holding the darkness outside at bay, comes the central "Time Passes" section of the novel, in which darkness and chaos rule, while human events, even the death of Mrs. Ramsay, are relegated to parenthetical comments. The experience of impermanence, change, and loss is underscored by the backdrop of the First World War in the middle section.

The novel's third section, "The Lighthouse," marks an attempted return to the pastoral setting of "The Window," but the return is qualified, even undercut, by the intervening chaos, darkness, and loss. The tension between the pastoral world view of "The Window" and the bleak world view of "Time Passes" becomes the subject matter of "The Lighthouse," as the extremes of the first two sections of the novel meet in the third section's return to the house without Mrs. Ramsay. James Ramsay's memory of "a garden where there was none of this gloom" is qualified by the intrusion of the recalled image of a "waggon" that crushes, "ignorantly and innocently, some one's foot" (*TL*, 275–76). And when Lily Briscoe finally sets out to finish the painting she had begun in "The Window," a painting that was to include Mrs. Ramsay, she faces in the empty drawing room steps the grief and loss at the heart of life: "Suddenly, the empty drawing room steps, the frill of the chair inside, the puppy tumbling on the terrace, the whole wave and whisper of the garden became like curves and arabesques flourishing round a centre of complete emptiness" (*TL*, 266). But out of this experience of emptiness in the garden, out of the reconciliation of the pastoral affirmation and the dark, chaotic negation, is born Lily's artistic vision.

Delta Wedding, Welty's first response to *To the Lighthouse*, lacks this ecstatic reconciliation because in Welty's novel the questioning of the pastoral is neither as open nor as central. The pastoral world view predominates throughout. In fact, Welty explains that she specifically chose to set *Delta Wedding* in a year without catastrophes, such as the First World War, that would intrude into the pastoral setting:

But in writing about the Delta, I had to pick a year—and this was quite hard to do—in which all the men could be home and uninvolved. It couldn't be a war year. It couldn't be a year when there was a flood in the Delta because those were the times before the flood control. It had to be a year

that would leave my characters all free to have a family story. It meant looking in the almanac—in fact, I did—to find a year that was uneventful and that would allow me to concentrate on the people without any undue outside influences; I wanted to write a story that showed the solidity of this family and the life that went on on a small scale in a world of its own. (*C*, 49–50)

Welty's comment here acknowledges the fragility of the pastoral world. For all of pastoral's assumption of a timeless harmony and balance through a close tie with the natural world represented by the garden, the natural world is also characterized by change and possible disaster. In many of Welty's other works, the natural world is anything but ordered and harmonious. The lake of "Moon Lake" is inhabited by snakes and the site of a near drowning; the climate of *Losing Battles* is dry and barren; the garden in "A Curtain of Green" resists all of the widowed Janey's attempts to discover order and harmony. Nature, in much of Welty's fiction, is, in Ruth Vande Kieft's words, "nature unpruned, uncultivated, formless in its fecundity."[8]

But in *Delta Wedding*, Welty's critique of the pastoral vision remains for the most part below the surface of the family idyll, never erupting in the chaos and destruction of Woolf's "Time Passes" section, and is noticed by only a few characters who keep their knowledge to themselves. The main threats to the family's security and peace—the near accident on the train trestle and Robbie and George's marital problems—remain just that: threats. The novel begins and ends in the safe, closed world of Shellmound, and Dabney's wedding underscores (indeed, almost parodies) the pastoral mode: the bridesmaids carry shepherds' crooks crowned with flowers and wear dresses the color of roses. This early Welty novel glances at the contradictions and repressions necessary to support a pastoral vision but does not engage on an explicit textual level the inconsistencies that become central concerns in her later novels. The lack of an overt critique of the pastoral world of the novel may account for the highly critical reviews that greeted the novel on its publication in 1946. Diana Trilling condemns the lack of social criticism in the novel's portrait of southern culture, arguing that Welty "leaves her honest cultural ob-

8. Vande Kieft, *Eudora Welty* (rev. ed.), 16.

servations in rosy poetic solution exactly because she does not wish to precipitate them as moral judgment." And as Ruth Vande Kieft points out, John Crowe Ransom's praise of Welty's novel in "Delta Fiction" is qualified by his concern that the novel lacks a certain political consciousness.[9] Yet if the pastoral world is not shattered as in *To the Lighthouse,* it has been qualified by the end of *Delta Wedding* by intrusions that occur throughout the novel. The bleak vision of "Time Passes" and the tentative resolutions of "The Lighthouse" become the repressed or marginalized elements, like Julia Kristeva's feminine, pre-symbolic elements, that disrupt the text and challenge the symbolic order of *Delta Wedding*'s pastoral patriarchal system.[10]

In both *To the Lighthouse* and *Delta Wedding,* the most conscious questioning of the pastoral vision on the part of a character comes, ironically, from the maternal, nurturing figures. Though Mrs. Ramsay and Ellen Fairchild stand at the center of their respective novels' affirmations of life, their personal, unspoken contemplations are generally not optimistic. While Mr. Ramsay verbally extends his self-pity to the rest of the world, muttering, "Poor little place," Mrs. Ramsay thinks to herself, "All this phrase-making was a game . . . for if she had said half what he said, she would have blown her brains out by now" (*TL,* 106). In the midst of the pastoral setting, she contemplates "suffering; death; the poor" (*TL,* 92). Similarly, Ellen Fairchild is the one in *Delta Wedding* who clearly sees the fear, contradiction, and denial implicit in her family's legend of happiness, and wishes "worse predicaments, darker passion, upon all their lives" (*DW,* 166).

As in *To the Lighthouse,* love and death go hand in hand in *Delta Wedding,* calling into question the pastoral innocence and optimism implied in the wedding of the novel's title. This connection is emphasized by the death of the anonymous young woman whose appearance in the bayou woods just a few days before Dabney's wedding touches Ellen Fairchild with fear for her family. In her brief talk with the girl, Ellen Fairchild tries to warn her of the link between sexuality and danger: "I

9. Diana Trilling, "Fiction in Review" (review of *Delta Wedding*), *Nation,* May 11, 1946, p. 578; Vande Kieft, *Eudora Welty* (rev. ed.), 85.

10. See Julia Kristeva, "Phonetics, Phonology, and Impulsional Bases," trans. Caren Greenberg, *Diacritics,* IV (Fall, 1974), 33–37; Moi, *Sexual/Textual Politics,* 166.

wasn't speaking about any little possession to you. I suppose I was speaking about good and bad, maybe. I was speaking about men—men, our lives" (*DW*, 71). After making love with George Fairchild, the girl is killed by the train that earlier had stopped short of killing him and Maureen Fairchild. Bringing tragedy so close to the charmed world of Shellmound, the episode of the mysterious girl stresses how precarious that charmed, protected quality is and qualifies the pastoral affirmation of love and marriage, suggesting the dangers that lie beneath the idyllic surface—dangers that are far more serious for women than men.

The pastoral affirmation of marriage is further disrupted in *Delta Wedding* by George and Robbie Fairchild's relationship. Though Robbie, having left George a few days earlier, does return to her husband in time for Dabney's wedding, their marital problems are not resolved by the novel's end, casting a faint shadow on the pastoral tableau of Dabney and Troy's wedding. Another Shellmound resident, Maureen, daughter of the deceased Denis Fairchild and his wife, Virgie Lee, serves as a reminder of a more tragic marriage. Though little is revealed about the marriage, Virgie Lee's spurning of the Fairchilds and her wild appearance reveal a degree of pain not acknowledged at Shellmound. Maureen, whose mental and emotional disturbances the family ignores, provides further testimony to the experience of violence and suffering that the pastoral world seeks to repress.

Virgie Lee and Maureen are also victims of larger tragedies the family denies. Though *Delta Wedding* is set between the two world wars and does not directly confront the chaos and destruction of war in the way that *To the Lighthouse* does, the tragedy of war hovers in the novel's margins, not only in the legends of the men who marched off to fight and never returned, but also in the legacy of insanity among the women and children left behind. Denis, killed in World War I, left behind Virgie Lee and Maureen, each marked by a form of mental or emotional disturbance. Aunt Shannon has completely lost touch with present reality; in the midst of the Fairchilds' plenty, she inhabits a memory world of war and deprivation, and she speaks to husbands, brothers-in-law, and nephews killed long ago in various wars. Indeed, the tragedy of war could not have been far from Welty's consciousness while she was writing *Delta Wedding*. Welty began work on "The Delta Cousins" in 1942 and spent

the next four years transforming the story into the novel published in
1946; in other words, during World War II Welty wrote this novel set in
the hopeful years of peace between the wars.[11]

The strongest challenge *Delta Wedding* poses to the pastoral world
view arrives at Shellmound in the character of Laura McRaven. According to DiBattista, "*To the Lighthouse* is centered in the relation between the 'dead' mother and the 'lost' daughter." *Delta Wedding* reenacts
this drama with Laura, whose "mother had died in the winter" (*DW,* 3).
The novel presents us with that loss in the first paragraph—"Poor Laura,
little motherless girl" (*DW,* 3)—and we carry it with us into the pastoral
world of Shellmound as we arrive there with Laura. Franziska Gygax
notes that Laura's association with tragedy is reflected in her name: "The
names Mc*Raven* and *Fair*child also reflect the difference between her
character and that of the host family. She is the dark girl from a place the
others do not care about." Reminders of Laura's loss recur throughout
the novel, momentarily fragmenting the enclosed, stable world of Shellmound where, as Peggy Whitman Prenshaw points out, "Death . . . contains few horrors, so easily does it yield to the assurance of nature's repeating cycles."[12] For Laura, and thus for the reader, the wedding itself
serves as a reminder of her mother's death: "The very breath of prepa-
ration in the air, drawing in or letting out, hurried or deep and slow,
made Dabney's wedding seem as fateful in the house as her mother's
funeral had been" (*DW,* 54). The connection between the wedding and
the funeral, between marriage and death, is further emphasized comically
when Miss Bonnie Hitchcock sends to the wedding the same enormous
fern she had sent over for Laura's mother's funeral.

Laura finds her grieving thwarted by the Fairchild attitude toward
death:

> Why couldn't she think of the death of her mother? When the Fairchilds
> spoke so easily of Annie Laurie, it shattered her thoughts like a stone in the
> bayou. How could this be? When people were at Shellmound it was as if

11. Kreyling, *Author and Agent,* 95.

12. DiBattista, *The Fables of Anon,* 76; Gygax, *Serious Daring from Within,* 19;
Prenshaw, "Woman's World, Man's Place," in *A Form of Thanks,* ed. Dollarhide and
Abadie, 49.

they had never been anywhere else. It must be that she herself was the only one to struggle against this. . . . And it was as if they had considered her mother all the time as belonging, in her life and in her death (for they took Laura and *let* her see the grave), as belonging here; they considered Shellmound the important part of life and death too. All they remembered and told her about was likely to be before Laura was born, and they could say so easily, "Before—or after—Annie Laurie died . . . ," to count the time of a dress being made or a fruit tree planted. (*DW,* 133–34)

Laura's questions challenge the Shellmound repression of loss and grief. Like Lily Briscoe in "The Lighthouse," Laura must experience and come to terms with her loss before she can move forward to the future. She must refuse the Fairchild denial of loss and reclaim her grief in order to recover her mother. The grief and the recovery occur simultaneously as Laura remembers her mother making the doll Marmion for her after returning to Jackson from a trip to Shellmound. Prenshaw notes that the "heightened tone of the prose suggests the drama of childbirth."[13] For Laura it marks the birth of the future out of the past, the birth of freedom out of memory. Laura's vivid memory of her mother provides the only physical description of Annie Laurie in the novel and creates Laura's strongest sense of connection with a world outside of Shellmound. At the same time, it brings Laura's sharpest sense of her loss as she realizes that "never more would she have this, the instant answer to a wish, for her mother was dead" (*DW,* 233). But this very awareness frees Laura to leave the magic, enclosed Fairchild world. Just a few pages later Laura feels a secret awareness that "in the end she would go—go from all this, go back to her father" (*DW,* 237). The sense of loss is linked to process, change, and the future in contrast to the stasis, the constant present, of the pastoral dream.

The vividness of Laura's memory of her mother brings her mother to life in the text in the same way that Lily's memory of Mrs. Ramsay recovers Mrs. Ramsay's presence: "There she sat" (*TL,* 300). "Like a work of art" (*TL,* 240), says Lily of her memory. Memory and art are

13. Prenshaw, "Woman's World, Man's Place," in *A Form of Thanks,* ed. Dollarhide and Abadie, 51.

closely connected in *To the Lighthouse;* indeed, memory of someone lost, bringing together presence and absence in one moment of experience, generates Lily's vision and her art, as well as the text's ultimate resolution. In *Delta Wedding,* however, this paradox of presence and absence remains a subtext unacknowledged by the primary narrative.

Threats of change in *Delta Wedding's* closing picnic and reunion scene foretell an approaching end to the unchanging, pastoral retreat of Shellmound. George's joking threat to oust his spinster sisters from their home, the Grove (whose very name evokes a pastoral eternity), and to return to live there himself disrupts the unity of the family picnic. His talk with Troy of growing vegetables and raising cows rather than growing cotton threatens to alter the plantation lifestyle.[14] These threats remind us that the novel is set in 1923, not in some pastoral, plantation past, and bring the novel's world into closer contact with the everyday reality that Welty, as well as Bakhtin, considers the province of the novel.[15] In "Place in Fiction," she remarks, "Fiction is properly at work on the here and now, or the past made here and now" (*E,* 117). Although the threats to the pastoral do not overwhelm Welty's narrative as they do in *To the Lighthouse,* they form one of the most important dialogues in Welty's novel. Like "the noiseless vibration that trembled" in the handle of Laura's china cup (*DW,* 17), Welty's critique of the pastoral rumbles beneath the pastoral quality of her story.

SUBJECTIVE AND CONCENTRIC NARRATIVES

Whereas Woolf's text overtly feminizes or novelizes the pastoral, challenging its nostalgic stasis and closed world and bringing it into dialogue with the very forces of change and chaos it seeks to repress, in Welty's text these forces remain marginalized. At the same time, Welty chose for this novel a narrative structure that calls attention to these margins. A

---

14. See Barbara Ladd, "Coming Through: The Black Initiate in *Delta Wedding,*" *Mississippi Quarterly,* XLI (1988), 541.

15. See Jan Nordby Gretlund, *Eudora Welty's Aesthetic of Place* (Newark, 1994), 156. Gretlund points out that Welty intentionally draws attention to the novel's time setting through her many references to songs, novels, movies, and fashion.

many-voiced narrative structure is another essential feature of both *To the Lighthouse* and *Delta Wedding*. Speaking of Welty's handling of point of view in *Delta Wedding*, Michael Kreyling calls this novel Welty's "major discovery of the technique that has sustained her as a novelist." [16] Kreyling refers here to the technique of distributing point of view among a variety of narrative consciousnesses that characterizes much of Welty's fiction. In both *To the Lighthouse* and *Delta Wedding*, narrative voice is fragmented; the narrative's authority is thereby decentered in a way that challenges the patriarchal insistence on unity and identity.

This fragmenting of point of view and of narrative authority exploits the novel's heteroglossia. Virginia Woolf's choice of such a narrative structure arose in part from her conscious rejection of a narrative form that imposed a fixed, authorial, monologic control of meaning. This rejection forms the subject of her essay "Mr. Bennett and Mrs. Brown," in which Woolf criticizes novelists H. G. Wells, John Galsworthy, and Arnold Bennett for imposing their social and literary programs upon the novel. She complains that in Bennett's novels we cannot hear the voices of the characters, but only "Mr. Bennett's voice telling us facts about rents and freeholds and copyholds and fines" (*CE, I,* 330). By giving "voices" to her characters and allowing them to "speak," Woolf recognized and used the possibilities of the novel's many-voiced form. Bakhtin explains that the "language used by characters in the novel, how they speak, is verbally and semantically autonomous; each character's speech possesses its own belief system, since each is the speech of another in another's language." Because each language within the novel's heteroglossia represents a different view of the world and provides a way of "conceptualizing the world in words," meaning is never single and fixed; it exists in the dialogue, on the boundaries between languages. [17]

Woolf in *A Room of One's Own* connects this splitting of the authorial "I" with the problem of writing as a woman in a male-dominated culture:

16. See Gygax, *Serious Daring from Within,* 37. In her discussion of the early negative reviews of *Delta Wedding*, Gygax argues, "It is only through the narrative strategy that the reader comes to realize that the depiction of Southern life in Shellmound neither lacks social criticism nor is 'morally discriminating' as has been stated by some critics"; Kreyling, *Eudora Welty's Achievement of Order,* xvi.

17. Bakhtin, *The Dialogic Imagination,* 315, 292.

"Again if one is a woman one is often surprised by a sudden splitting off of consciousness, say in walking down Whitehall, when from being the natural inheritor of that civilization, she becomes, on the contrary, outside of it, alien and critical" (*ROO*, 101). Considered in light of Toril Moi's argument that "the seamlessly unified self" represents the patriarchal desire to "banish from itself all conflict, contradiction and ambiguity," this narrative strategy seems especially appropriate for novels questioning gender assumptions, as it foregrounds conflict, contradiction, and ambiguity, and celebrates multiplicity and richness.[18]

It is precisely this many-voiced narrative strategy that Welty praises in her foreword to *To the Lighthouse:* "What Virginia Woolf has us see is the world as apparent to them—to Mrs. Ramsay, to Lily Briscoe, to James, Andrew, and the rest of the characters. From its beginning, the novel never departs from the subjective. The youngest child, James, is on page one cutting out a catalogue picture of a refrigerator which he sees 'fringed with joy.' The interior of its characters' lives is where we experience everything. And in the subjective—contrary to what so many authors find there—lies its clarity."[19] Welty chose this same "interior" mode for her first novel. *Delta Wedding*, like *To the Lighthouse*, opens with a child's world view and voice, as nine-year-old Laura McRaven journeys alone to visit her relatives. Upon Laura's arrival at Shellmound, the novel's point of view shifts to that of Ellen Fairchild, as the narrative begins its progression from voice to voice, never departing from what Welty calls "the subjective."

Within this narrative mode, gestures, objects, and events form patterns of meaning and significance only through the filter of characters' perceptions as their voices struggle and play against each other. Speaking of Woolf's novel, Welty notes that the lighthouse signals something different to each character and even something different to the same character at different times: "To some of the children [the lighthouse] remains as a father's promise of destination, a promise that a tyrant of a father can break, or can withhold until it's too late to make amends. To Mrs. Ramsay it is indeed her husband's promise to her children and is as well, in plain

18. Moi, *Sexual/Textual Politics*, 8.
19. Welty, Foreword to *To the Lighthouse*, viii.

fact, the home of the little boy with the tuberculous hip and the keeper, who regularly needs to be sent coffee, tobacco, warm stockings, and something to read."[20] We could easily expand this list. For Mrs. Ramsay, the lighthouse represents life, the loss of life, or at least of individuation, and even her own sense of self, of identity, as a process: "She looked up over her knitting and met the third stroke and it seemed to her like her own eyes meeting her own eyes, searching as she alone could search into her mind and her heart" (TL, 97).

The train trestle incident in Delta Wedding, in which George Fairchild and his mentally and emotionally disturbed niece, Maureen, narrowly miss being run down by the Yellow Dog, becomes a focal point similar to Woolf's lighthouse, the center of a ring of perspectives. For Ellen Fairchild it represents George's position vis à vis the family and the family's avoidance of tragedy. For Dabney, the bride-to-be, the incident is the prelude to her engagement, the dramatic event that precipitates Troy Flavin's proposal. Robbie Fairchild, George's wife, sees betrayal in George's actions, crying, "George Fairchild, you didn't do this for me!" (DW, 61). The oldest daughter, Shelley, sees in the near accident the fragility and threat in life; other members of the large, extended family neutralize the possibility of death and harm by incorporating the accident into the family mythology. Neither the lighthouse nor the train trestle can be reduced to one fixed and determinant meaning. Meaning becomes process rather than stasis. Presented through a variety of languages and world views, the event or symbol is thus "shot through with dialogized overtones."[21]

Carolyn Williams describes Woolf's "unique mode of narration" as "a concentric system with 'points of view' ranging around a character whose consciousness also penetrates outward in every direction" and compares her narrative technique to "a wheel whose axis and periphery may alternately be reached by many spokes of narrative access."[22] While this could pass as a general description of Welty's narrative technique in Delta Wedding as well, Woolf and Welty use the technique differently, and

20. Ibid., viii–ix.

21. Bakhtin, The Dialogic Imagination, 279.

22. Carolyn Williams, "Virginia Woolf's Rhetoric of Enclosure," Denver Quarterly, XVIII (1984), 49.

the differences have profound implications for their examinations of gender. Which characters are given voices in the narrative and which remain silent, closed off, and inaccessible is one significant difference between the two novels; the difference between the centers of each narrative circle is another important divergence.

Woolf uses this concentric narrative system in the "Window" and "Lighthouse" sections of *To the Lighthouse* to explore the issues of marriage, of women's and men's roles, and even masculine and feminine thought processes. Mr. Ramsay's mind divides thought into the letters of the alphabet, but Mrs. Ramsay, leaving analytical thought to her husband and sons, rests in the "admirable fabric of the masculine intelligence" (*TL,* 159), and seeks to know instead by "losing personality" (*TL,* 96) and merging with things outside herself. Whereas the masculine conception of self is single, autonomous, and unitary, the feminine conception of self in this novel is contextual and multiple. Though the text may privilege women's voices—Mrs. Ramsay's in the first section and Lily Briscoe's in the third—the narrative also enters into the consciousnesses of male characters, of Mr. Ramsay, James Ramsay, William Bankes, and Charles Tansley. Because *To the Lighthouse* employs what we might call an "androgynous" narrative, one that can enter the minds and emotions of both men and women, we hear all sides in the dialogue between masculine and feminine perspectives.

At the center of the concentric narrative system in *To the Lighthouse* is Mrs. Ramsay. She clearly stands (or sits) at the heart of the "Window" section, providing the focal point for the other characters' thoughts and emotions, and her voice predominates throughout the novel's first section as she contemplates herself and her relation to others. In "The Lighthouse" she is still at the center, though absent; the other characters define themselves in relation to her absence. Her voice echoes throughout the section's imagery until she is finally made present in Lily's painting and vision. And even in "Time Passes," where the world exists stripped of human perception, she is central, as her death is mirrored in the outbreak of war and the disintegration of the house. The section itself becomes a textual enactment of her absence.

In *Delta Wedding,* however, the narrative perspective is filtered through female characters only, principally Laura McRaven and Shelley, Robbie,

and Ellen Fairchild. Men's and boys' voices are heard only in the outwardly spoken dialogues among the characters; their few spoken words are framed by the women's and girls' perspectives, which provide the context in which we hear and understand the masculine discourse. The narrative never fully reflects a masculine consciousness. Instead of the feminine silences feminist criticism has taught us to expect, Welty's novel dramatizes masculine silence and inaccessibility. Though the novel questions the masculine world and perspective through the voices of the women and girls who observe it, such questions remain unanswered: the masculine voice remains silent, and the masculine world remains a mystery. Shelley Fairchild ponders this mystery after watching Troy Flavin, her sister's fiancé and the plantation overseer, handle the threat of violence on the part of a field hand: "Suppose the behavior of all men were actually no more than this—imitation of other men. But it had previously occurred to her that Troy was trying to imitate her father. (Suppose her father imitated . . . oh, not he!) Then all men could not know any too well what they were doing" (DW, 196).

Welty uses this narrative strategy to reenact the gender division of Shellmound as the women and girls there experience it. Even little Laura McRaven knows that "the boys and the men . . . defined the family always. All the girls knew it" (DW, 14). When she contemplates the Fairchild boys, Laura sees them as a group, despite their varied ages. She notes that they are "constantly seeking one another, even at the table with their eyes, seeking the girls only for their audience when they hadn't one another" (DW, 13). Though Laura feels shut out by the boys, she defines her identity in relation to them and considers India, her closest girl cousin, "second best": "She loved them dearly. It was strange that it was India who had to be Laura's favorite cousin, since she would have given anything if the boy cousins would let her love them most. Of course she expected them to fly from her side like birds, and light on the joggling board, as they had done when she arrived, and to edge her off when she climbed up with them. That changed nothing" (DW, 14). Laura sees herself and India as outsiders, as other than the defining principle in this world. Because they are female, Laura and India are marginalized observers of masculine activity.[23]

23. See Danielle Fuller, "Making a Scene: Some Thoughts on Female Sexuality and

Within the novel's world, women silently question this marginalized arrangement. As Shelley Fairchild understands, "Everything [women] knew they would have to keep to themselves" (*DW,* 196). Within the text, however, women do not keep quiet. Welty gives them the voices denied them by the world of the Fairchild family and foregrounds their marginalized observations and comments. In other words, Welty's narrative strategies in *Delta Wedding* subvert Shellmound's silencing of women by allowing them to speak those things they "have to keep to themselves." Thus, rather than merely representing the patriarchal voice of authority, Welty's novel draws the patriarchal discourse into a dialogue with the marginalized female voices in order to open the dominant voice to questioning and revision.

One of the ways in which the novel gives a voice to woman's traditionally silenced knowledge is through the textual interruptions of Shelley Fairchild's diary and Ellen Fairchild's dreams, both traditionally private, "feminine" genres that Welty uses to disrupt the narrative's unity and linearity. Through her diary entries, Shelley challenges the patriarchal discourse of Shellmound and resists its insistence on marriage as she watches her sister Dabney "walk into something you dread and you cannot speak to her" (*DW,* 85). Not surprisingly, Shelley's liberating engagement with language and the private pleasure she finds in the word are restricted by her father:

> There was no way on earth Shelley could get a lamp brought in to read by in bed. A long brass pole dangled from the center of the ceiling ending in two brass lilies from each of which a long, naked, but weak light bulb stuck out. "Plenty of light to dress by, and you can read in the lower part of the house with your clothes on like other people," Uncle Battle said, favoring Dabney as he did and she never read, not having time. A paper kewpie doll

Marriage in Eudora Welty's *Delta Wedding* and *The Optimist's Daughter*," *Mississippi Quarterly,* XLVIII (1995), 296. Fuller argues persuasively that despite the novel's foregrounding of women, the novel depicts "a matriarchy surrounded by and embedded in—both literally and metaphorically—a 'plantation discourse' that confirms the social and economic power of white males of the middle and upper classes."

batted about on a thread tied to the chandelier, that was all it was good for.
. . . It was hard for her to even see how to write. (*DW,* 83)

The violent and sexual imagery of the naked lightbulbs and the batted
kewpie doll suggests a connection between sexual difference and the
struggle over language. By insisting that Shelley's engagement with language take place in the context of family life, her father seeks to tame
and restrict the pleasure that Shelley finds in her writing. But Welty's
inclusion of Shelley's diary entry subverts and thwarts such a restriction.
The text gives a voice to the feminine commentary that the novel's patriarchal world seeks to silence and deny.

Ellen Fairchild's dreams form another example of the text's privileging
of feminine commentary and genre. In fact, the text gives the dreams a
validity that Ellen herself doubts: "She often told dreams to Bluet at
bedtime and nap time, for they were convenient—the only things she
knew that were not real" (*DW,* 65). But Ellen silently "trust[s] her
dreams," and the text confirms their truth: "She dreamed the location
of mistakes in the accounts and the payroll that her husband—not born
a business man—had let pass, and discovered how Mr. Bascom had
cheated them and stolen so much; and she dreamed whether any of the
connection needed her in their various places, the Grove, Inverness, or
the tenants down the river, and they always did when she got there"
(*DW,* 65).

Reverberations of the dream she describes to Bluet—a warning about
the loss of a garnet pin—can be felt disturbingly throughout the narrative. This dream propels Ellen toward her meeting with the young girl
in the woods, an encounter in which "a whole mystery of life opened
up" (*DW,* 70). The girl is a nymph figure whose mythic, "poetic" beauty
is enhanced by "the soiled cheek, the leafy hair, the wide-awake eyes"
(*DW,* 71). The garnet pin becomes an emblem of feminine sexuality in
their brief and enigmatic conversation. When the girl protests, "Nobody
can say I stole no pin," Ellen replies, "I wasn't speaking about any little
possession to you. I suppose I was speaking about good and bad, maybe.
I was speaking about men—men, our lives" (*DW,* 71). She points out
the road toward Memphis, "the old Delta synonym for pleasure, trouble,
and shame" (*DW,* 72). The narrative enacts the threat that the patriarchal

world poses to women when later in the novel this beautiful girl, whom George Fairchild met and "slept with" in "the old Argyle gin" (*DW,* 79), is killed by a train. Her mutilated body is captured by the camera of the wedding photographer, underscoring the relationship between feminine sexuality and violence. Later in the novel Ellen's dream and its warning recur in the experience of Laura McRaven, who finds the garnet pin in the woods near Marmion: "It was a pin that looked like a rose. She knew it would be worn here—putting her forefinger to her small, bony chest" (*DW,* 177). But Laura is still a child, not yet ready for the pleasure or danger of sexuality, and she loses the pin again almost immediately. The warning of Ellen's dream is once again fulfilled, and feminine sexuality remains hidden and repressed.

Even though the text voices women's thoughts and experiences through these various strategies, men remain the focus of women's attention and the subject of much of their discourse: "Men—our lives" (*DW,* 71). The narrative structure places George Fairchild, a man whose psyche the narrative does not enter, at the center of the concentric pattern of feminine voices and visions of *Delta Wedding.*[24] George is the character whom the women of the Fairchild family question, consider, praise, and punish, as the characters of *To the Lighthouse* do Mrs. Ramsay. For Ellen, the "near-calamity on the trestle was nearer than she had realized to the heart of much that had happened in her family lately" (*DW,* 157), and George is at the center of that incident. Dabney sees Uncle George as "the very heart of the family" (*DW,* 33). Laura McRaven feels that the cousins "all crowded him so . . . and she would have liked to clear them away, give him room" (*DW,* 76). Further complicating matters is the narrative's association of George with his dead brother Denis, raising questions about presence and absence, and with the masculine myth of Dionysus. John Alexander Allen claims, "If one had to pick the Greek god that George resembles . . . it would surely be Dionysus. The association of that god with literal and emotional intoxication, with ecstatic states combined with abundant kindness, fits George's char-

24. For brief references to the narrative's exclusion from the male characters' thoughts, see Vande Kieft, *Eudora Welty* (rev. ed.), 72; Gygax, *Serious Daring from Within,* 38.

acter and role exactly. Like Dionysus, George is attuned to all realities, including death."[25] Right before Ellen faints, she sees George with "his shoulders as bare . . . as a Greek god's, his hair on his forehead as if he were intoxicated, unconscious of the leaf caught there, looking joyous" (*DW,* 166).

The text thus encircles the masculine with the feminine; the male principle is enclosed within the female. Images of enclosure abound in *Delta Wedding* as the women define themselves in relation to this masculine center. Laura observes the insider/outsider dynamic of the Fairchilds as a form of enclosure when she and the other girls play "Go in and out the window": "It was funny how sometimes you wanted to be in a circle and then you wanted out of it in a rush. Sometimes the circle was for you, sometimes against you, if you were It. Sometimes in the circle you longed for the lone outsider to come in—sometimes you couldn't wait to close her out. It was never a good circle unless you were in it, catching hands, and knowing the song. A circle was ugly without you" (*DW,* 73). The motif of pregnancy offers other examples of enclosure. Pregnant, Ellen's body encloses a child that will look like Battle: "She had never had a child to take after herself and would be as astonished as Battle now to see her own ways or looks dominant, a blue-eyed, dark-haired, small-boned baby lying in her arms" (*DW,* 22). Mary Denis Summers Buchanan's baby is a boy with flaming red hair like his father's.

This connection of enclosure with pregnancy suggests a specifically feminine form of creativity.[26] Enclosure provides the women of *Delta Wedding* a way of resolving the self/other, masculine/feminine dichotomy. Impenetrable mystery and otherness are enclosed and placed at the center of Welty's concentric patterns in *Delta Wedding.* Out of an encounter with this mystery comes a sense of self as process and change, of becoming. Laura's initiation experience at Marmion is full of these images of enclosed mystery that reverberate with sexuality. Aunt Studney (her name suggesting masculine sexuality) appears at Marmion with her

25. John Alexander Allen, "The Other Way to Live: Demigods in Eudora Welty's Fiction," in *Critical Essays,* ed. Prenshaw, 29.

26. Weston, *Gothic Traditions and Narrative Techniques,* 3, notes "the theme of enclosure and escape" runs throughout Welty's fiction; Weston associates it with the Gothic form's renegotiation of gender and power.

mysterious sack out of which, says Roy, "Mama gets all her babies" (*DW,* 173). The room Laura and Roy enter at Marmion is round, "the inside of a tower" (*DW,* 174). As Laura and Roy run "around and around the round room," Aunt Studney stands in the center and turns "herself in place around and around, arms bent and hovering, like an old bird over her one egg" (*DW,* 175). In Laura's immersion in the Yazoo, the river of death, she enters into the interior of this mystery: "As though Aunt Studney's sack had opened after all, like a whale's mouth, Laura opening up her eyes head down saw its insides all around her—dark water and fearful fishes" (*DW,* 178). This baptism marks a turning point for Laura in her relationship to the Fairchilds. Paradoxically, enclosure leads to growth and expansion for Laura.

This "rhetoric of enclosure" that connects feminine creativity, self-definition, and narrative structure is one that Woolf used in *To the Lighthouse,* according to Carolyn Williams. Uniting Lily Briscoe's artistic vision and the structure of *To the Lighthouse,* Williams offers this explanation:

> But what arises as an invocation of loss, emptiness, and vacancy takes shape and form around that center. Emptiness generates form in these Woolfian elegies, and form depends upon emptiness at the center. . . . Characterization and narrative form are subtly linked in Woolf's novels, and one way to discover the variety of these relations is to notice the same concentric structures being used as figures for identity, for life in the body, and for narrative form. I want to emphasize these relations and at the same time to suggest, among the many contexts available for placing Woolf's "rhetoric of enclosure," an approach that would pointedly attempt to situate it as a rhetoric specifically of female embodiment.[27]

If emptiness and loss lie at the center of Woolf's forms, mystery— masculine and sexual—lies at the heart of Welty's *Delta Wedding.*

We could read this structure as one in which women are marginalized, while men stand at the center, determining meaning and structure. But I believe that Welty's fiction goes beyond this limiting interpretation that

27. Williams, "Virginia Woolf's Rhetoric of Enclosure," 46–47.

ultimately reinforces the dominant discourse. Jacques Derrida's comments on the center are useful here in reading and interpreting Welty's structure: "The concept of center was not only to orient, balance, and organize the structure—one cannot in fact conceive of an unorganized structure—but above all to make sure that the organizing principle of the structure would limit what we might call the play of the structure." Derrida further notes that "at the center, the permutation or the transformation of elements is forbidden."[28] As the center of the family and the novel, the Fairchild men are the origin and the epitome, but they are also fixed and static. The men repeat themselves generation after generation: Laura McRaven "from her earliest memory had heard how they 'never seemed to change at all' " (*DW,* 15). Not only do the masculine generations represented in the library paintings look identical, but they are conflated into a single, unified "Somebody" in the family stories: "That was Somebody's gun . . . and Somebody's pistol in the lady's workbox . . . Somebody's Port Gibson flintlock, and Somebody's fowling piece" (*DW,* 98). At the same time that the center is the "organizing principle of the structure," it is also the static and limiting element; in the margins the women exist in a state of play, of process and becoming. In other words, Welty transforms women's marginalized status into an emancipatory and creative space where women can question and revise the patriarchal discourse of the family. Thus Shelley's diary and Ellen Fairchild's dreams and visions portending loss and tragedy rupture and qualify the pastoral, patriarchal claim of Fairchild happiness and the seductive innocence of the novel's authoritative community.

Still, the ending of *Delta Wedding* is ambivalent. The novel closes in traditional comic form with a family picnic to celebrate the return of the newlywed couple, Dabney and Troy. But beneath this celebration of the patriarchal myth of pastoral order and happiness lie foreboding tensions. The song the family sings, "Oh, you'll take the high road and I'll take the low road," suggests separation and hierarchy. Laura's sleepy speculations stress loss and division: "They're singing to Uncle George that his wife has left him. . . . And to Dabney that she and Troy will never meet again" (*DW,* 241). Although Welty has created a narrative structure that

28. Jacques Derrida, *Writing and Difference,* trans. Alan Bass (Chicago, 1978), 278–79.

foregrounds marginalized voices and questions the supremacy of patriarchal and pastoral myths and assumptions, those myths and assumptions
remain intact at the novel's close, though the challenges to the pastoral
patriarchy rumble beneath the surface. If, as Hélène Cixous claims, "A
feminist text cannot fail to be more than subversive. It is volcanic," Welty's
Delta Wedding is a text that resides on the verge of erupting.[29]

Woolf's use of pastoral elements and a concentric narrative structure
in *To the Lighthouse* provided Welty with some of the raw material for
her first full novel, *Delta Wedding*. Woolf's text is one of the voices that
inhabits Welty's novel. And like Woolf, Welty uses these narrative strategies to consider and evaluate gender assumptions and relationships in her
novel's world. But in this early work, Welty shies away from the radical
perspective of Woolf's novel. Whereas the artist's transformative vision
concludes *To the Lighthouse,* Welty provides no artist in *Delta Wedding*
whose vision, like Lily Briscoe's, can encompass, question, and dismantle
the traditional, repressive hierarchies of gender opposition. Toril Moi
describes the importance of Lily Briscoe's artistic vision to Woolf's novel:
"*To the Lighthouse* illustrates the destructive nature of a metaphysical belief
in strong, immutably fixed gender identities—as represented by Mr. and
Mrs. Ramsay—whereas Lily Briscoe (an artist) represents the subject
who deconstructs this opposition, perceives its pernicious influence and
tries as far as is possible in a still rigidly patriarchal order to live as her
own woman, without regard for the crippling definitions of sexual identity to which society would have her conform."[30]

The closest we get to an artist in Welty's first novel is little Laura
McRaven, through whose eyes the narrative paints the vivid opening
scenes of the Delta. Laura can draw, as the narrator mentions twice. The
first time, Laura is commenting on the landscape outside her train window: "The land was perfectly flat and level, but it shimmered like the
wing of a lighted dragonfly. It seemed strummed, as though it were an
instrument and something had touched it. Sometimes in the cotton were
trees with one or two or three arms—she could draw better trees than

29. Hélène Cixous, "The Laugh of the Medusa," in *New French Feminisms,* ed. Elaine
Marks and Isabelle de Courtivron, trans. Keith Cohen and Paula Cohen (New York,
1981), 258.

30. Moi, *Sexual/Textual Politics,* 13.

those were" (*DW*, 4). The juxtaposition of the shimmering dragonfly's wing with drawing echoes Lily Briscoe's desire for her painting: "Beautiful and bright it should be on the surface, feathery and evanescent, one colour melting into another like the colours on a butterfly's wing; but beneath the fabric must be clamped together with bolts of iron" (*TL*, 255).

The second reference to Laura's drawing occurs in her recollection of the dollmaking, here linking memory and art: "Laura leaned on her mother's long, soft knee, with her chin in her palm, entirely charmed by the drawing of the face. She could draw better than her mother could and the inferiority of the drawing, the slowly produced wildness of the unlevel eyes, the nose like a ditto mark, and the straight-line mouth with its slow, final additions of curves at the end, bringing at maddening delay a kind of smile, were like magic to watch" (*DW*, 232).

As an outsider and observer who has experienced the grief and loss the Fairchilds seek to deny, and as an adventurer who knows "about geography," Laura comes closer to being an artist figure than any other character in *Delta Wedding*. But she is only nine years old and hardly mature enough to provide the novel with the same sort of ecstatic, revolutionary vision Lily Briscoe gives *To the Lighthouse*. Laura McRaven is, however, the forerunner of several artist figures appearing in Welty's later fiction: Cassie Morrison and Virgie Rainey in *The Golden Apples*, the storytelling women of *Losing Battles*, and Laurel McKelva Hand in *The Optimist's Daughter*, Welty's second response to *To the Lighthouse*. With a name so similar to Laura McRaven's, Laurel McKelva Hand is an artist who offers the counterpart to Lily Briscoe missing in *Delta Wedding*. Only when Welty returns again to the patterns of *To the Lighthouse* in writing *The Optimist's Daughter* does she fully address the vision of the "Time Passes" and "Lighthouse" sections of Woolf's novel.

II

HISTORICAL FANTASIES
AND FANTASTIC HISTORIES
The Robber Bridegroom and *Orlando*

E VEN before Eudora Welty wrote *Delta Wedding*, an imaginative interaction with Virginia Woolf's fiction marked her work. Two of
Welty's letters to Katherine Anne Porter indicate that Welty was reading Woolf's fiction in 1941 and 1942 during the debate over where
to publish *The Robber Bridegroom*.[1] In a 1941 letter Welty writes, "Virginia
Woolf's last book just came today and I am about to read it. Have you
read it? There is so much to be done, just slave work, in the house and
yard, that I have the book set up on end, slightly opened, like a reward,
on my table, a promise that I can read it tonight if I don't cheat." In a
letter dated summer, 1942, the year she began writing "The Delta Cousins," Welty describes one of her rereadings of *To the Lighthouse*: "Since
I've been home I haven't done anything but a little flower-watering and
book-reading—I mostly stay in bed and swallow quinine, though the
fevers run up and down paying no attention. Now they are down, and
I hope for good. I read 'To the Lighthouse' again, which in some ways
is the most beautiful to me of all Virginia Woolf's books."[2]

In *The Robber Bridegroom*, Welty makes extensive use of "The Fisherman and His Wife," the same Grimm brothers' fairy tale that Virginia

1. Kreyling, *Author and Agent*, 62–66, describes the difficulties Welty had placing
The Robber Bridegroom.
2. Eudora Welty to Katherine Anne Porter, 1941, in Katherine Anne Porter Collection, McKeldin Library, University of Maryland, Baltimore; Welty to Porter, Summer,
1942, *ibid.*

Woolf uses in *To the Lighthouse*. This fairy tale recounts the adventures of a fisherman who catches and releases an enchanted flounder. When he returns home to the pigsty in which he and his wife live, his wife insists that he go back to the sea and ask the flounder to give them a cottage. The flounder grants her wish, but the wife soon grows discontented and demands that her husband ask the flounder for a castle. Her greed and desire for power prompt her to demand a series of gifts from the flounder, who makes her king, then emperor, then pope. Finally, when she wishes to be God, the flounder returns the couple to their original state of poverty in the pigsty.[3]

Interpreted from a feminist perspective, this fairy tale tells the story of a strong-willed woman denied any outlet for action in the world except through the agency of her weaker-willed husband. "Well, what does she want, then?" asks the flounder, as if a woman's wanting were in itself too much, a form of presumption. In Woolf's *To the Lighthouse*, Mrs. Ramsay reads "The Fisherman and His Wife" to her son James while engaging in a silent power struggle with her husband. The Grimm brothers' narrative punctures the pastoral romance of "The Window." Although Mr. Ramsay wields the ostensible power in the Ramsays' marriage, Mrs. Ramsay seeks to control him by withdrawing into herself and refusing to tell him she loves him. She turns women's traditional passivity and compliance against him. Mr. Bankes's suggestion that Mr. Ramsay compromised a brilliant career for his marriage further complicates the sexual and romantic politics of this section. Denied the means to act in the masculine world, to reform dairies and found hospitals, Mrs. Ramsay is reduced, like the fisherman's wife, to manipulating her husband and her children: "Wishing to dominate, wishing to interfere, making people do what she wished—that was the charge against her" (*TL*, 88).

Salome Musgrove, in Eudora Welty's *The Robber Bridegroom*, shares a more obvious affinity with the grasping wife of the fairy tale. Indeed, in "Fairy Tale of the Natchez Trace," Welty tells us that Salome should remind the reader of "The Fisherman and His Wife" (*E*, 304). Like the fisherman's wife, Salome knows the frustration of being married to a

---

3. Jakob Grimm and Wilhelm Grimm, *Grimms' Tales for Young and Old: The Complete Stories*, trans. Ralph Manheim (New York, 1977), 70–76.

man less ambitious than she. Never content with what she possesses, always seeking wealth and aggrandizement through her husband, Salome tells Clement that she will not be satisfied until they live in "a mansion at least five stories high, with an observatory of the river on top of that, with twenty-two Corinthian columns to hold up the roof" (*RB,* 100). Because she cannot enter the sphere of masculine action and acquisition like Clement and Jamie Lockhart, Salome expends her calculating energy pushing Clement into action and scheming against his daughter, Rosamond, trying to pit her and Clement against each other. Like Woolf, Welty uses these echoes of "The Fisherman and His Wife" to puncture a pastoral myth. In *The Robber Bridegroom,* she uses references to the fairy tale to reveal the dark underside of what Michael Kreyling describes as "the pursuit of a chimeric, pastoral, fundamentally American Eden." [4] Fueling the conquering and developing of the American wilderness in Welty's fictional rendition is the uncontrolled greed and dissatisfaction represented by Salome's desires.

In *The Madwoman in the Attic,* Sandra Gilbert and Susan Gubar claim that the double portrait of woman as angel and monster that is seen in Rosamond and Salome, or Mrs. Ramsay and the fisherman's wife, is central to our culture's mythology of women and central to our fictions. They argue that "patriarchal texts have traditionally suggested that every angelically selfless Snow White must be hunted, if not haunted, by a wickedly assertive Stepmother: for every glowing portrait of submissive women enshrined in domesticity, there exists an equally important negative image that embodies the sacrilegious fiendishness of what William Blake called the 'Female Will.'" [5]

Virginia Woolf and Eudora Welty explore this dichotomy and the power of the "Female Will" by incorporating a traditional patriarchal text, a fairy tale, into their novels in a manner that raises questions about the values and world view implicit in the fairy tale.[6] Blake's "Female

4. Kreyling, *Eudora Welty's Achievement of Order,* 34.

5. Gilbert and Gubar, *The Madwoman in the Attic,* 28.

6. Jack Zipes, *Fairy Tales and the Art of Subversion: The Classical Genre for Children and the Process of Civilization* (New York, 1983), 7. Zipes describes the *patriarchalization* of fairy tales: "By the time the oral folk tales, originally stamped by matriarchal mythology, circulated in the Middle Ages, they had been transformed in different ways: the goddess

Will," if used for woman's defense or increase, is seen as a usurpation of masculine power and is characterized by extreme negative qualities: greed, lust for absolute power, and presumption. The fisherman's wife longs to be like God, Salome challenges the sun, and Mrs. Ramsay sees life itself as her antagonist. "Female Will" violates the patriarchal order; fairy tales exact a punishment that restores power to the masculine domain and leaves the woman at least powerless, often dead. Although the fisherman's wife simply returns to her original impoverished and powerless state, Salome Musgrove, like Snow White's wicked stepmother, dances herself to death. Once she is dead, her power reverts back to the patriarchal order. Salome is reduced to a physical body, a mere possession: "What man," asks the chief of the Indian tribe, "owns the body of this woman?" "'I do,' said Clement. 'I own her body'" (RB, 164).

Mrs. Ramsay dies as well, though the more severe punishment exacted in *To the Lighthouse* is the constant killing off of self, the repression of identity, that constitutes the powerful woman's daily existence within the male-dominated culture. The call to suppress her strength of will, to defer to and bolster her husband, leaves Mrs. Ramsay with "scarcely a shell of herself left for her to know herself by" (TL, 60). References to the Grimms' fairy tale underscore Mrs. Ramsay's guilt at feeling her own strength and power:

> Yet, as the resonance died, and she turned to the Fairy Tale again, Mrs. Ramsay felt not only exhausted in body . . . but also there tinged her physical fatigue some faintly disagreeable sensation with another origin. Not that, as she read aloud the story of the Fisherman's Wife, she knew precisely what it came from; nor did she let herself put into words her dissatisfaction when she realized, at the turn of the page when she stopped and heard dully, ominously, a wave fall, how it came from this: she did not like, even for a second, to feel finer than her husband. (TL, 61)

---

became a witch, evil fairy, or stepmother; the active, young princess was changed into an active hero; matrilineal marriage and family ties became patrilineal; the essence of the symbols, based on matriarchal rites, was depleted and made benign; the pattern of action which concerned maturation and integration was gradually recast to stress domination and wealth." The characteristics of patriarchal fairy tales that Zipes catalogues are those that Woolf and Welty call into question in their novels.

Cultural narratives such as the fairy tale repeatedly warn women of the dangers of such strengths. But by incorporating the fairy tale into her novel, Woolf draws it into a dialogue that questions such warnings and the gender restrictions they work to enforce.

Salome's dance of death is not the only reference to "Snow White" in *The Robber Bridegroom*. Salome, as the evil stepmother, sees the innocent Rosamond as her opponent in a rivalry based, as in "Snow White," on youth and beauty: "For if Rosamond was as beautiful as the day, Salome was as ugly as the night" (*RB*, 33). Because she cannot enter the sphere of masculine action and acquisition like Clement and Jamie Lockhart, Salome expends her energy scheming against Clement's daughter, represented as a fairy-tale heroine. Rosamond "has every fairy tale property," explains Welty in "Fairy Tale of the Natchez Trace." She is "beautiful and young and unwed, with a devoted father and a wicked stepmother, and she is also an heiress" (*E*, 305). Salome sends Rosamond on a fairy-tale errand, to "the fartherest edge of the indigo field, on the other side of the woods, [to] gather the herbs that grow there" (*RB*, 37). But Rosamond remains untouched by the dark woods and herbal metaphors of feminine power. Like Snow White, she leaves her father's house and the torments of her stepmother to become housekeeper for a group of men. Later in the story, as Peter Schmidt explains, "Rosamond makes the transition from having to care for a host of unruly males to having a home of her own with one husband and the prospect of a nuclear family."[7] In this pattern, Rosamond follows in the footsteps of her fairy-tale predecessors.

The most violent scene in *The Robber Bridegroom*, Little Harp's violation and murder of an Indian woman, comes straight out of another fairy tale, the Grimms' "The Robber Bridegroom," also Welty's source for the novel's title. In the fairy-tale version, a young girl is betrothed to a man she neither loves nor trusts. When she visits his house in the forest, a caged bird tells her she has come to a murderer's house, and an old woman warns her that the robbers who live there, led by her betrothed, plan to kill, cook, and eat her. The bride hides behind a barrel and watches as the robbers drug, kill, and devour another young woman. As

7. Schmidt, *The Heart of the Story*, 129.

they chop the girl's body to pieces, her little finger flies into the bride's lap. The bride escapes and on her wedding day denounces the robber bridegroom to the wedding party by revealing the murdered girl's finger. The robber bridegroom and his band are put to death.[8] Suggesting that the traditional plot for women—courtship and marriage—ends in destruction, not fulfillment, this fairy tale enacts marriage's consumption of a woman. Like the Grimms' young bride-to-be, Rosamond watches from behind a barrel as Little Harp kills the Indian woman and catches the woman's severed finger in her lap. Through Welty's textual references to the fairy tale, Rosamond figuratively experiences the female victim's literal consumption by the masculine plot.

Despite all the fairy-tale features of *The Robber Bridegroom*, Welty's novel is not itself a fairy tale, as Lionel Trilling suggested in "American Fairy Tale," his 1942 review of the book. In "Eudora Welty's Parody," Marilyn Arnold argues that the novel is a parody of a fairy tale: "Using what appears on the surface to be standard characters and motifs, Welty creates standard expectations in the reader; but she does not fulfill them. Instead, she subverts, reverses, burlesques, and just generally scatters asunder the fairy tale's sacrosanct notions about the agenda for happily-ever-after living."[9] Welty herself, in "Place in Fiction," draws a marked distinction between the province of fairy tale and novel: "There are only four words, of all the millions we've hatched, that a novel rules out: 'Once upon a time.' They make a story a fairy tale by the simple sweep of the remove—by abolishing the present and the place where we are instead of conveying them to us. . . . Fiction [unlike the fairy tale] is properly at work on the here and now, or the past made here and now; for in novels *we* have to be there" (*E*, 117).

Welty's novel is much more than a fairy tale; indeed, fairy tales are just one of the genres Welty incorporates into *The Robber Bridegroom*. Upon opening the novel, the reader enters a maze of intertextuality, a looking-glass world, in which Eudora Welty weaves together the characters, plots, and languages of history, folk tale, fairy tale, and myth.

8. Grimm and Grimm, *Grimms' Tales for Young and Old*, 146–49.

9. Lionel Trilling, "American Fairy Tale," *Nation*, December 19, 1942, p. 687; Marilyn Arnold, "Eudora Welty's Parody," in *Critical Essays on Eudora Welty*, ed. Turner and Harding, 33.

Though intertextuality is a characteristic of *To the Lighthouse,* a more fruitful novel to study in dialogue with the imaginative world of *The Robber Bridegroom* is Virginia Woolf's *Orlando* (1928). Lionel Trilling noted the affinity between these two works in a highly critical review. "In short," complains Trilling, Welty "has written one of those fabrications of fantasy which have so tempted two other gifted women of our time—Elinor Wylie with her 'The Venetian Glass Nephew' and her 'Mr. Hazard and Mr. Hodge,' and Virginia Woolf with her 'Orlando,' very artful and delicate works, very remote and aloof, though passionately connected, in secret ways, with the lives of the authors themselves, and very exasperating in their inevitably coy mystification." [10]

As Trilling's complaint demonstrates, *Orlando* and *The Robber Bridegroom* occupy similar positions in each writer's canon and pose similar problems for critics. The authors' comments suggest that these novels also sprang from similar moods and motives and that their composition processes shared the same spirit. Woolf calls the writing of *Orlando* "a writer's holiday" (*WD,* 122) and describes the joyous ease with which she wrote it: "How extraordinarily unwilled by me but potent in its own right, by the way, *Orlando* was! as if it shoved everything aside to come into existence. Yet I see looking back just now to March that it is almost exactly in spirit, though not in actual facts, the book I planned then as an escapade; the spirit to be satiric, the structure wild. Precisely" (*WD,* 118). Echoing Woolf's language, Welty calls her novel "as wild as anything." [11] Her comments on composing *The Robber Bridegroom* reveal the same excitement and energy: "I had such a good time writing it! I had been working for the WPA or for the Mississippi Advertising Commission. In the course of my work I had to do a lot of reading on the Natchez Trace. I'm not a writer who writes fiction by research, but reading these primary sources, such as Dow's sermons, Murrell's diary and letters of the times, fired my imagination. I thought how much like fairy tales all of those things were. And so I just sat down and wrote *The Robber Bridegroom* in a great spurt of pleasure" (*C,* 24).

10. Trilling, "American Fairy Tale," 687.
11. Eudora Welty to Katherine Anne Porter, February 15, 1941, in Katherine Anne Porter Collection.

Perhaps it is this element of fun in *The Robber Bridegroom* and *Orlando* that has led so many critics to ignore or slight these two works, treating them as less important than or even unconnected to the writers' other novels. Jean Love describes *Orlando* as "something of an anomaly among Virginia Woolf's novels," claiming that it is "not tightly bound to her other books, not quite as continuous with them as they are with each other. Rather, it is marked by its ties to her life, not her other novels." Whereas some critics have considered *Orlando* only in terms of Virginia Woolf's or Vita Sackville-West's biography, others simply sidestep the novel, treating it less fully than Woolf's other works. In her essay, "Why Is *Orlando* Difficult?" J. J. Wilson briefly traces the critical neglect of *Orlando:* "'Brilliant but incongruous,' says Mitchell Leaska, thus explaining its omission from his *The Novels of Virginia Woolf: From Beginning to End.* Another ambitiously titled book, *Feminism and Art,* seems almost to overlook *Orlando,* a work one would think central to the topic. James Naremore treats it out of sequence, with *Between the Acts,* and thus misses the significance of its timing in Woolf's development. A. D. Moody mutters, 'It would be difficult to say at all simply what it is about,' devoting to the task only half a paragraph." [12]

Welty's *The Robber Bridegroom* has suffered similar neglect or misunderstanding, especially by early critics. Lionel Trilling criticized it for lacking seriousness and for being too simple. "Nothing," he claimed, "can be falser, more purple and 'literary' than conscious simplicity." Ruth Vande Kieft's 1962 edition of *Eudora Welty* and Alfred Appel, Jr.'s *A Season of Dreams: The Fiction of Eudora Welty,* devote only a few pages to *The Robber Bridegroom.* Appel comments incorrectly that its comic spirit is "seldom qualified by irony." [13]

Those critics who do take *Orlando* and *The Robber Bridegroom* seriously often seem puzzled about how to classify these works. Joanne Trautmann describes Woolf's novel as "a parody of biography, an essay in the exotic,

---

12. Jean Love, "*Orlando* and Its Genesis: Venturing and Experimenting in Art, Love, and Sex," in *Virginia Woolf: Revaluation and Continuity,* ed. Ralph Freedman (Berkeley, 1980), 192; J. J. Wilson, "Why Is *Orlando* Difficult?" in *New Feminist Essays,* ed. Marcus, 170.

13. Trilling, "American Fairy Tale," 687; Alfred Appel, Jr., *A Season of Dreams: The Fiction of Eudora Welty* (Baton Rouge, 1965), 51.

a mock-heroic novel of ideas, an imaginative literary and social history of England, and a biography of V. Sackville-West." Maria DiBattista adds to this list "a private joke," "a public comedy of historical and literary manners," and "a pan-historical fantasy satirizing sex roles, literary styles, social fashions, and political factionalism." J. J. Wilson goes even further, calling *Orlando* an "anti-novel" and claiming as its ancestry "Chaucer's *Tale of Sir Thopas, Don Quixote,* much of Shakespeare and Rabelais, Austen's *Northanger Abbey,* Carlyle's *Sartor Resartus,* Mark Twain's *Connecticut Yankee in King Arthur's Court.*"[14]

Too long for a short story but somewhat short for a novel, Welty's *The Robber Bridegroom* is difficult to categorize. The list of genres critics have identified in it is as impressive as the list compiled for *Orlando.* Welty herself names the components of Mississippi history, story-telling traditions, fairy tales, and myths (*C,* 189). To her list Michael Kreyling adds "folk tale, legend, fantasy, blood violence" and traces *The Robber Bridegroom*'s lineage in the American novel, arguing that "like *The Blithedale Romance* or *The Great Gatsby, The Robber Bridegroom* balances the futility of pursuing the pastoral ideal against the necessity for dreaming it." Both Ashley Brown and Robert L. Phillips, Jr., call *The Robber Bridegroom* a romance. Warren French claims that *The Robber Bridegroom* shares features with "the 'Newgate pastoral' of the bourgeois ascendancy in England," while Charles Davis argues more convincingly for "the author's use of the tradition of the Old Southwest humorists."[15]

Despite (or perhaps because of) their generic uncertainty, both *Orlando* and *The Robber Bridegroom* are integral works in their authors' canons. Jean Guiguet argues convincingly for *Orlando*'s continuity with Virginia Woolf's other novels in spite of its lighthearted tone and ironic

14. Joanne Trautmann, "*Orlando* and Vita Sackville-West," in *Critical Essays on Virginia Woolf,* ed. Morris Beja (Boston, 1985), 99; DiBattista, *The Fables of Anon,* 111; Wilson, "Why Is *Orlando* Difficult?" in *New Feminist Essays,* ed. Marcus, 172–73.

15. Kreyling, *Eudora Welty's Achievement of Order,* 49; Ashley Brown, "Eudora Welty and the Mythos of Summer," *Shenandoah,* XX (Spring, 1969), 29; Robert L. Phillips, Jr., "A Structural Approach to Myth in the Fiction of Eudora Welty," in *Critical Essays,* ed. Prenshaw, 61; Warren French, "All Things Are Double: Eudora Welty as a Civilized Writer," in *Critical Essays,* ed. Prenshaw, 187. Charles Davis, "Eudora Welty's *The Robber Bridegroom* and Old Southwest Humor: A Doubleness of Vision," in *A Still Moment: Essays on the Art of Eudora Welty,* ed. John F. Desmond (Metuchen, N.J., 1978), 71.

manipulation of genres: "Thus *Orlando* cannot be confined within any of the genres in which it participates, and . . . we have to recognize it as a novel of the same type, if not in the same vein, as the rest of Virginia Woolf's novels. Like them it rejects literary conventions, and like them it seeks, with apparent casualness but in all sincerity, to grasp the essence of a fluid and complex reality which our habits of speech, confused with our habits of thought, have unduly solidified and simplified."[16] Like *To the Lighthouse*, *Orlando* explores gender relationships, feminine subjectivity, and the woman as artist, as well as the nature of reality and the nature of the novel. With its seamless shifts between the worlds of realism and fantasy, Eudora Welty's *The Robber Bridegroom* is perhaps the clearest tie between Welty's novels and her short stories. It shares many themes with *Delta Wedding*, the novel that followed it, including an exploration of gender assumptions, female initiation, women as writers, and the problems inherent in a pastoral view of reality.

In addition to sharing a playful energy, an exuberance that makes them a delight to read, and being integral works in their authors' canons, *Orlando* and *The Robber Bridegroom* have much else in common. Reading Welty's early novel as a Bakhtinian response to Woolf's *Orlando* offers new insights into this often-neglected work by Welty. Both works offer a complex exploration of identity, especially feminine identity, posing questions about the construction of subjectivity and its relationship to historical context and cultural narratives. Both works experiment with a mixture of genres, some literary and some extraliterary, thus extending the boundaries of the novel as a genre. Intertextuality in these two novels becomes a way of reinventing literary forms and traditions so that they accommodate woman and allow her to speak, to narrate her life and tell her own stories. Using irony, comedy, and parody as narrative strategies, these are feminist novels that cross boundaries, resist hierarchy, defy categories, and embrace paradox, contradiction, and disruption.

FEMININE NARRATIVES

Both *Orlando* and *The Robber Bridegroom* explore the mystery of human personality, asking questions about identity and self-definition. What

16. Guiguet, *Virginia Woolf and Her Works*, 266.

does identity consist of? Is it fixed, constant, and unified, or fluid and multiple? How much of an individual's identity depends on historical setting, on place and time? How much depends on gender? On social and family setting? On genre? Virginia Woolf addresses these concerns through *Orlando*'s historic and literary overview of England. Passing through the various phases of English history—Renaissance, Enlightenment, Victorian, modern—the main character, Orlando, changes with the age, adapting—or at least trying to—to the spirit of each period. As a Renaissance man, Orlando is serious, lusty, violent, and passionate. As an Enlightenment woman, Orlando becomes witty, reasoning, and social. As a Victorian woman, Orlando feels weighted down by the age and marries to comply with its demands. Nick Greene changes as well, from the sardonic, querulous Renaissance poet who rails about "Glawr" to the eminent Victorian critic, a plump, sleek, prosperous pedant.

Eudora Welty's *The Robber Bridegroom,* though covering a significantly shorter time span, is set during the American westward expansion, a time of rapid social and cultural change. As Welty says of the time in which the novel is set, "Life was so full, so excessively charged with energy in those days, when nothing seemed impossible in the Natchez country, that leading one life hardly provided scope enough for it all" (*E,* 310–11). In the course of the narrative, the central "figure of the age" changes from hunter to planter to merchant, and as Clement Musgrove comes to realize, each type will have its rise and fall. The identity of many characters in Welty's novel depends specifically on the cultural and historical milieu. The passing of time reduces Mike Fink, legendary flatboatman, to anonymity, while Jamie Lockhart adapts, changing with the times from bandit to merchant.

Orlando's comprehensive experience and memory of English history alienates her from any specific era. Her larger, distanced perspective allows her to see herself in time and to perceive the self as changing and always becoming. Identity, in *Orlando,* is process rather than stasis. This distanced stance allows Orlando to see that the "truths" her culture accepts as absolutes are actually social and linguistic constructions that remain vulnerable to change. Judy Little argues that "moving through an open-ended history of open-ended sentences that vary with the style of the age (and which themselves style or write the age), Orlando must

continually revise perceptions about everything from his early passion for Sasha, to the style of his or her poem 'The Oak Tree.' Even such pervasive cultural codes as fame, human nature, and gender, which a given spirit of an age will see as absolute, Orlando learns to see as illusion, as something unspoken."[17] The spirit of the age in *The Robber Bridegroom*, the frontier spirit of the American westward expansion, is equally suspect. It is constructed in the same way that Mike Fink constructs the legend of himself, through exaggeration and storytelling. But like Jamie Lockhart, the age seeks to repress the darker side of the conquest of nature and indigenous populations. Either way, suggests Welty's text with its mixture of genres, history is as much a linguistic construction, a form of storytelling, as fairy tale and legend. In the context of *The Robber Bridegroom*, history becomes another of the stories we tell ourselves in order to construct our cultural and individual identities.

Contemplating the mystery of identity, Clement Musgrove asks, " 'What exactly is this now?' . . . For he too was concerned with the identity of a man, and had to speak, if only to the stones" (*RB*, 141). Both Virginia Woolf and Eudora Welty are concerned as well in these novels with the identity of a woman. Woolf's *Orlando* is very obviously a novel about gender and self-definition. She examines the masculine and feminine elements in both the culture and the individual and the significance of gender in the construction of identity. The novel connects Orlando's striving for intellectual development and social freedom to his/ her growth as a writer. Thus, Woolf links writing to gender and self-definition, and the struggle to achieve freedom as a woman becomes part of Orlando's struggle to discover or create a literary voice in which to write her own story. Welty's *The Robber Bridegroom* responds to many of the issues of *Orlando*. On the level of plot and theme, Welty approaches these concerns less directly than Woolf. *The Robber Bridegroom* could almost be called a novel of thwarted female self-definition: the social constraints against women's intellectual and moral development prevail more thoroughly in *The Robber Bridegroom* than in *Orlando*, and the female

17. Judy Little, "(En)gendering Laughter: Woolf's *Orlando* as Contraband in the Age of Joyce," in *Last Laughs: Perspectives on Women and Comedy*, ed. Regina Barreca (New York, 1988), 185.

characters' attempts to control the narratives that shape their lives are less successful than Orlando's. On a textual level, however, Welty's dialogic narrative challenges these social and narrative constraints, offering a playful and liberating alternative vision.

In *Orlando,* Virginia Woolf specifically creates a character conscious of the social roles and values assigned to women. Because Orlando is not born a woman but becomes one only after spending thirty successful years as a man, she possesses a distance and detachment from the culture's feminine roles that few "from birth" women can achieve. For "if one has been a man for thirty years or so, and an Ambassador into the bargain, if one has held a Queen in one's arms and one or two other ladies, if report be true, of less exalted rank, if one has married a Rosina Pepita, and so on" (*O,* 154), then one cannot enter without hesitation and self-consciousness into the culture's feminine roles, attitudes, and domains.

In the comic scene in which Orlando awakens as a woman from a long, mysterious sleep, the figure of Truth banishes the Ladies of Purity, Chastity, and Modesty, traditional guardians of a woman's honor. In Chapter 4, however, covering Orlando's return to England after a sexually undifferentiated "childhood" with the band of gypsies, Orlando is very rapidly initiated into the demands and limitations of her new sexual identity. She discovers the social importance and restraint of purity, chastity, and modesty. The journey by ship across a large body of water serves as a metaphoric, mythic initiation into the woman's world. Orlando contemplates "the penalties and the privileges of her position" (*O,* 153); although she discovers that nothing "is more heavenly than to resist and to yield" (*O,* 155), most of her thoughts incline toward the limitations of her new identity. She discovers that "the sacred responsibilities of womanhood" include, in addition to keeping her legs covered "lest a sailor may fall from a mast-head" (*O,* 157), a number of other sacrifices and limitations she had not known as a man:

> "And that's the last oath I shall ever be able to swear," she thought, "once I set foot on English soil. And I shall never be able to crack a man over the head, or tell him he lies in his teeth, or draw my sword and run him through the body, or sit among my peers, or wear a coronet, or walk in procession, or sentence a man to death, or lead an army, or prance down Whitehall on

a charger, or wear seventy-two different medals on my breast. All I can do, once I set foot on English soil, is to pour out tea, and ask my lords how they like it. D'you take sugar? D'you take cream?" (*O*, 157–58)

A woman's identity, suggests Woolf, is defined negatively, by what she cannot do. As the ship lands in England, Orlando takes an even bleaker view of her new destiny, thinking that, "however much landing there meant comfort, meant opulence, meant consequence and state (for she would doubtless pick up some noble Prince and reign, his consort, over half Yorkshire), still, if it meant conventionality, meant slavery, meant deceit, meant denying her love, fettering her limbs, pursing her lips, and restraining her tongue, then she would turn about with the ship and set sail once more for the gipsies" (*O*, 163).

But because Orlando has spent thirty years as a man and is not, therefore, unconsciously and thoroughly defined with reference to gender, she has access to a degree of mental, emotional, and even physical freedom not available to other women in the novel. Similarly, because the realities of biological time do not constrain Orlando, whose life spans centuries rather than decades, she is not fully bound or defined by the mores and values of any specific age. Though she feels more at ease in some historical periods and more oppressed in others, she remains detached from and even critical of each age. Just as the late transition from man to woman makes her aware of the constructed quality of gender identities that are usually part of one's unconscious, "naturalized" cultural experience, so her continual transition from one age to another keeps her in a state of conscious cultural initiation. The novel thus suggests that the concept of an individual self separate from a cultural context is a fiction and emphasizes the degree to which identity depends on its particular historical setting. Because of the constant changing of cultural context, in Woolf's novel subjectivity is necessarily shifting and multifaceted rather than fixed and unitary. It is, notes Christy Burns, "depicted as a mesh of various optional identities." Asks Orlando, "How many people are there not—Heaven help us—all having lodgment at one time or another in the human spirit?" (*O*, 308).[18]

18. Christy L. Burns, "Re-Dressing Feminist Identities: Tensions Between Essential and Constructed Selves in Virginia Woolf's *Orlando*," *Twentieth-Century Literature*, XL (1994), 358.

In Orlando's multifaceted, multigendered identity, Woolf dismantles the masculine-self/feminine-other hierarchy and resists a phallocentric insistence on identity as static and unitary. Her heroine's creative freedom depends upon a collaboration between the masculine and feminine facets of her personality. According to Woolf in *A Room of One's Own*, it is a state necessary to writing: "Some collaboration has to take place in the mind between the woman and the man before the act of creation can be accomplished. Some marriage of opposites has to be consummated. The whole of the mind must lie wide open if we are to get the sense that the writer is communicating his experience with perfect fullness" (*ROO*, 108).

Thus the process of self-definition is closely tied in Woolf's novel to Orlando's development as a writer. Like cultural identity, individual identity becomes a rhetorical and even literary construct. The history of her poem, "The Oak Tree," becomes the history of Orlando herself. Orlando's thoughts about writing and identity are sometimes so intertwined that the two become one and the same: " 'I will write,' she had said, 'what I enjoy writing'; and so had scratched out twenty-six volumes. Yet still for all her travels and adventures and profound thinkings and turnings this way and that, *she was only in process of fabrication*" (*O*, 175; emphasis added).

As Orlando matures, her feminine nature predominates. Maturing along with her, her narrative style becomes less ornate and bombastic. Orlando's switch from poetry to prose is presented in feminine images: "Slowly there had opened within her something intricate and many-chambered, which one must take a torch to explore, in prose not verse" (*O*, 175). The narrative style of the novel itself matures and grows more feminine as well. The novel's subject matter grows more serious and thoughtful as the narrative style and tone grow more internal and self-conscious in order to contemplate and express Orlando's experiences as a woman. Orlando's description of her prose is very similar to Woolf's description of her own writing process, her "tunnelling process." In her diary, Woolf describes this process, which she discovered while writing *Mrs. Dalloway:* "How I dig out beautiful caves behind my characters: I think that gives exactly what I want; humanity, humour, depth. The idea is that the caves shall connect and each comes to daylight at the present

moment" (*WD*, 59). Woolf's comment on Dorothy Richardson's feminine sentence is also illuminating in this context: "She has invented, or,
if she has not invented, developed and applied to her own uses, a sentence
which we might call the psychological sentence of the feminine gender.
It is of a more elastic fibre than the old, capable of stretching to the
extreme, of suspending the frailest particles, of enveloping the vaguest
shapes."[19] The language Woolf employs to describe "feminine writing"—"caves," "elastic," "extremes," "enveloping"—foreshadows the
language used by late-twentieth-century French feminist theorists such
as Hélène Cixous and Luce Irigaray.

Further emphasizing the tie between gender and writing, Orlando's
completion of "The Oak Tree," her life's work, is tied to the birth of her
son. As DiBattista notes, "Orlando's poetic quest begins, conventionally
enough, on the threshold of manhood and terminates, narratively, if not
psychologically, with the birth of a child, metaphorically linked to the
delivery of her manuscript after a long period of gestation."[20] The language used to describe the completed manuscript characterizes it as an
infant, "a being, who, though not herself, yet entirely depended on her"
(*O*, 272). The fulfillment of Orlando's poetic quest is thus tied to the
fulfillment of a specifically feminine creative potential, and writing is
transformed in the course of Woolf's novel from an adolescent, masculine
pastime into a mature, feminine act of creation. The traditional tension
between motherhood and authorship is resolved in the representation of
her text as her child. The text she creates is her own, is a woman's story
of process, a dialogue of discovery: "Was not writing poetry a secret
transaction, a voice answering a voice?" (*O*, 325).

Though *The Robber Bridegroom* considers the same intersection of gender, identity, and the creation of narratives, Welty's treatment of these
issues is often overlooked by critics who focus primarily upon the characters of Clement Musgrove and Jamie Lockhart, disregarding Salome as
the obstacle the hero must overcome and Rosamond as his reward for
prevailing. The issue of women as creators of their own stories is quite

19. Virginia Woolf, Review of Dorothy Richardson's *Revolving Lights,* in *Women
and Writing,* ed. Michele Barrett (New York, 1979), 191.

20. DiBattista, *The Fables of Anon,* 125.

complex in *The Robber Bridegroom*. The men in the novel actively define themselves through storytelling. "I'm a he-bull and a he-rattlesnake and a he-alligator all in one!" (*RB*, 10) insists Mike Fink, yoking narration, masculinity, and identity into a single declaration. Clement tells Jamie Lockhart "the story of his life" (*RB*, 20), while Jamie Lockhart carefully masks his identity by refusing to tell his own story. Unlike the men, who author their own lives and legends, Salome's and Rosamond's stories are controlled by men. It is Clement who narrates the tale of Salome's endless desire and capture by Indians and Clement who promises Rosamond to Jamie Lockhart in reward for finding the bandit who robbed her of her clothing. Whereas Virginia Woolf's Orlando is an author, Salome and Rosamond can be only covert storytellers: Salome's plotting to get rid of Rosamond and increase her own wealth and Rosamond's lying are among the disruptive forms of storytelling used by these women whose lives are dominated by men.

Salome plots to control her world. She directs Clement's successful enterprises since she cannot, as a woman, act on her own. Her plots mark her refusal to live out someone else's script and her attempt to inscribe her own. And no wonder: the other narratives open to women in *The Robber Bridegroom* are not very attractive. Goat's sisters seek matrimony so desperately that they are willing to marry a stranger with a "head no larger than something off the orange tree, . . . his forehead . . . full of bumps like an alligator's, and two teeth [sticking] out of his mouth like the broadhorns on a flatboat" (*RB*, 98). Within the cultural/historical context of the novel, matrimony is the only legitimate story for women. Outside of marriage lie tales of seduction, shame, and danger like that of the Indian woman raped and murdered—consumed—by Little Harp. The goals of Salome's plots, like those of the fisherman's wife, are power, choice, autonomy, and wealth—all characteristic of the masculine world of action. Denied the means for direct action in this world, Salome creates narratives, "plots" in which men, Clement or Goat, act for her. Ultimately, Salome meets her death as the result of an extreme attempt to exert narrative control over the world in which she lives. Challenging the Indians who hold her captive, she claims complete autonomy: "'No one is to have power over me!' Salome cried, shaking both her fists in the smoky air. 'No man, and none of the elements! I am by myself in

the world'" (*RB*, 160–61). But Salome loses her battle against the established patriarchal narratives that, like "Snow White," demand the punishment of a powerful and independent woman. Like the madwomen of Gilbert's and Gubar's study, Salome must be destroyed. She does not succeed in reinscribing a woman's narrative.

Rosamond, the "heroine" of *The Robber Bridegroom*, also uses a covert form of storytelling to subvert the patriarchal script in which she lives so powerlessly. Her lies form an attempt to rewrite the feminine roles dictated to her by her father and lover. Rosamond's lies, compared by the narrator to jewels, are precious to her: "When she opened her mouth in answer to a question, the lies would simply fall out like diamonds and pearls" (*RB*, 38–39). Her father, however, seeks to silence her attempts to rescript her life, declaring that "if a man could be found anywhere in the world who could make her tell the truth, he would turn her over to him" (*RB*, 39). The primary purpose of Rosamond's lies is self-protection, first from her stepmother who sends her out on dangerous errands, and later from Jamie Lockhart. Rosamond tells him that she has "a father who has killed a hundred Indians and twenty bandits as well, and seven brothers that are all in hearty health. They will come after you for this, you may be sure, and hang you to a tree before you are an hour away" (*RB*, 49). She lies again, in both words and behavior, to prevent being given in marriage as reward to a man she does not know. Later in the novel, she lies to gain release from the Indians. When Goat asks, "And will you let me come sleep in your little bed and be my wife?" (*RB*, 151), Rosamond replies "Yes!" The narrator then remarks, "It was lucky for her she did not have to learn to tell a lie there on the spot, but already knew how" (*RB*, 152).

In her lying, Rosamond seeks to rewrite the traditional narratives for women. Her responses to Jamie during the clothes-stealing scene and even her claim about her seven brothers come from the traditional ballad "Young Andrew." [21] Rosamond reworks in several ways this narrative of seduction and shame in which a young woman is seduced and rejected and then dies. Harriet Pollack argues rightly that "the pessimistic expec-

21. Gordon E. Slethaug, "Initiation in Eudora Welty's *The Robber Bridegroom*," *Southern Humanities Review*, VII (1973), 80–81.

tations that a reader might base on 'Young Andrew' are disappointed when Rosamond successfully recasts the melancholy ballad in a comic genre." [22] Rosamond rejects the traditional plot underlying the ballad, the plot that limits a young woman's choices to marriage and legitimacy or to seduction, shame, and death. Although Rosamond and the young woman of the ballad make the same choice—to return home rather than be killed by their seducers—the spirit and outcome of their choices are worlds apart. Young Andrew's victim returns home to a father who carries out the patriarchy's punishment of a "ruined" woman—death. Rosamond, however, "who had imagined such happenings in the world" (*RB,* 49) and enjoys "thinking of how she might look without a stitch on her" (*RB,* 50), replies without shame and with delightful common sense to Jamie Lockhart's question: " 'But wait,' he said, 'which would you rather? Shall I kill you with my little dirk, to save your name, or will you go home naked?' . . . 'Why sir, life is sweet,' said Rosamond, looking up straight at him through the two curtains of her hair, 'and before I would die on the point of your sword, I would go home naked any day' " (*RB,* 50). In Rosamond's revision of the ballad's seduction myth, the choice of death is ludicrous. Rosamond refuses to live (*or* die) according to the traditional script for women and uses her lies to create more desirable alternatives. [23]

Rosamond's imagination is full of fairy tales and ballads, of romantic plots that color her view of the world. But rather than accepting these plots unquestioningly, she chooses to tell her own story by recasting these plots in a positive key. She is, as Welty remarks, a fairy-tale character with "ironic modifications" (*E,* 306). Carolyn Heilbrun's comments on women's stories in "What Was Penelope Unweaving?" are illuminating in this context. Heilbrun remarks, "All women, having been restricted

22. Harriet Pollack, "On Welty's Use of Allusion: Expectations and Their Revisions in 'The Wide Net,' *The Robber Bridegroom,* and 'At the Landing,'" *Southern Quarterly,* XXIX (1990), 18.

23. Weston, *Gothic Traditions and Narrative Techniques,* 10, 178. Weston identifies Washington Irving's "Story of the Young Robber" as another of Welty's sources for *The Robber Bridegroom.* Irving's story, like the traditional ballad, ends with the father's "cold reply" to a ransom note from the young robber who then stabs the young woman to death.

to only one plot, are without story. In literature and out, through all recorded history, women have lived by a script they did not write. Their destiny was to be married, circulated; to be given by one man, the father, to another, the husband; to become the mother of men. Theirs has been the marriage plot, the erotic plot, the courtship plot, but never, as for men, the quest plot. . . . The question women must all ask is how to be freed from the marriage plot and initiated into the quest plot." Indeed, another function of Rosamond's lies is to allow her to step into the quest plot, where, as Heilbrun reminds us, "men might do anything," whereas women in the marriage plot "might only wait to be desired, to be wed, to be forgotten."[24] Rosamond does not remain at home waiting to be sought after, the passive object of masculine desire. "The fairy tale daughter," remarks Welty, "is also the child of her times, a straightforward little pioneer herself" (*E*, 307). She refuses to enact the pattern of being the reward for the heroic quest. Instead, she appropriates the quest plot, going on her own quest in search of Jamie: "She set out of the house, carrying a lunch of a small cake she had baked especially, to find where he lived" (*RB*, 76). She ignores the warning of the fairy-tale raven, enters the bandits' cave, and finds Jamie Lockhart, the object of her quest. But upon fulfilling her quest, Rosamond ends up back in, if not the marriage plot, at least the domestic plot. Jamie robs and plunders all day long, and she marks time cleaning, cooking, and mending for his band of robbers. Still, Rosamond attempts to order and record her life, if she cannot control it, by labeling and dating all of the "treasures" Jamie brings her—a "thousand pieces of English silver or the scalp of a Creek" (*RB*, 87).

The traditional narratives are hard to subvert, but Welty's text does not allow Rosamond to remain as the domesticating influence on the bandits. Her second quest is interwoven with Welty's allusions to the Psyche myth, commonly viewed as a pattern of female initiation and development. In Apuleius' version of the myth, Psyche draws Aphrodite's anger because mortals begin to celebrate Psyche's beauty and neglect Aphrodite's temples. But when the goddess sends her son, Eros, to punish Psyche, he falls in love with her instead and makes her his mistress. Forbidding her to ask who he is, forbidding her even to see his face, he

24. Carolyn Heilbrun, *Hamlet's Mother and Other Women* (New York, 1990), 108.

comes to her only under the cover of night and leaves her before dawn every morning. Psyche's jealous sisters convince her that her lover is a monstrous snake, thus tempting her to disobey his commands and look at him. Lighting a lamp while he sleeps, Psyche recognizes Eros and falls in love with him. But just as she discovers his identity, a drop of hot oil from the lamp awakens him, and he deserts her because of her disobedience and her knowledge.

To recover Eros, Psyche, now pregnant with his child, becomes a quester. She must undertake four tasks assigned by angry Aphrodite. The first three tasks she performs with help from the natural world. These tasks take her from the protected palace of Eros, from the dubious safety of the erotic plot, out into the world and lead her through a process of self-discovery to a stance of self-reliance. The final task takes her on a journey to the underworld to seek the secret of beauty from Persephone. Bringing back a casket of a special beauty potion, Psyche succumbs again to her desire for knowledge: opening the casket causes her to fall into an enchanted sleep from which Eros must rescue her. He wakes her, and Aphrodite finally approves their union. Psyche is made a goddess, and the divine world celebrates her marriage to Eros and the birth of their child, Pleasure.[25] In her essay, "Fairy Tale of the Natchez Trace," Eudora Welty ties the Psyche myth to the imaginative world of *The Robber Bridegroom:*

> Jamie's berry stains, the disguise in which he carries on his work, in which he kidnaps Rosamond, and in which he has continued to keep his identity secret from her after she joins him in the robbers' house (he never lets her see his face unwashed) are conventional in Mississippi history (the bandit Mason blackened his face as a disguise) and still more widely in song and story. Bandits, adventurers, lovers and gods have the disguise in common. But girls always fall for taking it off. Psyche, in the fable, held a candle over

25. Apuleius, *The Golden Ass,* trans. Robert Graves (New York, 1951), 96–143. See also Mary Anne Ferguson, "The Female Novel of Development and the Myth of Psyche," *Denver Quarterly,* XVII (1983), 62; Kenneth D. Chamlee, "Grimm and Apuleius: Myth-Blending in Eudora Welty's *The Robber Bridegroom," Notes on Mississippi Writers,* XXIII (1991), 38–42.

Cupid's sleeping face—a god who only came in the dark—then let a drop of hot wax fall, and up he jumped, away he flew. (E, 308)

Jamie and Rosamond reenact the myth of Eros and Psyche. Once Jamie kidnaps Rosamond, she lives with him happily except for one flaw: he will not allow her to see his face and to know his identity. Though he may see, know, and thus possess her, his mask of berry stains prevents her from knowing him, and he remains a mystery to Rosamond. In this state of ignorance, Rosamond is denied knowledge of her lover, of her world, and therefore of herself; her fear of losing Jamie overcomes her desire for knowledge. Welty's imagery connects Jamie's disguise to language and narrative: "Sometimes she would wake up out of her first sleep and study his sleeping face, but she did not know the language it was written in. And she would look out the window and see a cloud put up a mask over the secret face of the moon" (RB, 84–85). Rosamond not only does not write but also cannot even read the texts that control her life.

When she does manage to remove the berry stains, there occurs a moment of instantaneous recognition for both Rosamond and Jamie: "You are Jamie Lockhart!" cries Rosamond. "And you are Clement Musgrove's silly daughter!" replies Jamie (RB, 134). As in the story of Psyche, Rosamond's assertion of her desire for knowledge is viewed as an act of selfish disobedience: "Good-by," Jamie says. "For you did not trust me, and did not love me, for you wanted only to know who I am. Now I cannot stay in the house with you" (RB, 135). Rosamond's assertion of her desire for knowledge is construed as selfish, as a threat to patriarchal power and identity, and results in his abandoning her.

Just when Jamie abandons her, Rosamond discovers that she is pregnant: "At the same moment, she felt the stirring within her that sent her a fresh piece of news" (RB, 135). Welty's language ties pregnancy to discourse and the creative potential for self-knowledge. The text's focus shifts again at this point from the story of the Robber Bridegroom to the story of the Questing Bride. Pregnant, like Psyche, Rosamond must venture out into the world beyond the robbers' house to search for her lover. A textual "pioneer," Welty's heroine steps outside the passive female

role inscribed by the phallocentric text and into the quest narrative usually reserved for our culture's heros.

Rosamond once again succeeds in her quest; she finds Jamie Lockhart.
And there her story stops. Rosamond's final tale has a curiously rehearsed
sound, as though she tells someone else's story in someone else's language.
Supplanted by husband and children, she is no longer the subject of her
own story. Her lies now add color to her narrative—"a blue silk canopy"
(RB, 184)—but no longer subvert and revise the traditional plot. She
tells her father that she misses "the house in the wood, and even the
rough-and-tumble of their old life" (RB, 184). And no wonder; once
again the fulfillment of Rosamond's quest lands her back in the marriage
plot in which feminine identity becomes fixed and static. Living in wealth
in New Orleans, she has stepped out of the frontier setting that could
accommodate her courageous and adventurous qualities. No longer a
"little pioneer," she now fulfills the prescribed social role of wife and
mother. When Jamie thanks Clement for his daughter, their original
deal—Clement's daughter in exchange for Jamie's finding her—is completed. It does not matter that Rosamond actually found Jamie; the patriarchal script reduces her to a commodity. She has stepped outside of
the fairy-tale world of "happily ever after" and returned to the central
narrative for women—the narrative of exchange, marriage, motherhood—and no longer narrates her own story.

FEMINIZED NARRATIVES

As pioneers of the novel, Virginia Woolf and Eudora Welty are more
successful than Rosamond and Salome. Playing with forms of storytelling
and manipulating various traditional forms such as ballad, myth, and fairy
tale, both Orlando and The Robber Bridegroom are characterized by a generic uncertainty, a shifting and sliding of boundaries. Woolf and Welty
consciously manipulate other genres, incorporating them into their
novels in a manner that raises questions about the genres' conventions.
As Bakhtin suggests, the novel is the site of struggle among various languages and their ideologies. In Orlando and The Robber Bridegroom, the
languages and assumptions of the various genres interact with each other.

Because most traditional genres are phallocentric systems, it is precisely this sort of interaction among languages, claims Patricia Yaeger, that makes the novel attractive to women writers: "As a multivoiced, multi-languaged form—a form inviting the novelist to parody other discourses and portray a dialogic 'struggle among sociolinguistic points of view'—the novel is a genre that encourages its writers to assault the language systems of others and to admit into these language systems the disruptive ebullience of other speech and of laughter." [26]

Intertextuality provides women writers a way of appropriating masculine genres, a way of vocalizing repressed feminine voices, thus bringing the genres into a dialogue. As we have seen, *Orlando* and *The Robber Bridegroom* are novels about storytelling and about the restrictions various genres impose upon women. In their intertextuality, these novels manage to escape such restrictions and explore ways in which women writers can reinvent masculine literary traditions so that they accommodate women and allow them to speak.

Among the many genres Virginia Woolf plays with in *Orlando* are biography, literary history, national history, fantasy, *Bildungsroman,* myth, and philosophy. Eudora Welty's *The Robber Bridegroom* incorporates elements of history, fairy tale, fantasy, frontier legend, myth, Southwest humor, and American pastoral. Brought into the novel's field of uncertainty and becoming, these genres are, in Bakhtin's term, *novelized,* or *feminized* in the terms of feminist theories of language: "They become more free and flexible, their language renews itself by incorporating extraliterary heteroglossia and the 'novelistic' layers of literary language, they become dialogized, permeated with laughter, irony, humor, elements of self-parody and finally—this is the most important thing—the novel inserts into these other genres an indeterminacy, a certain semantic openendedness, a living contact with unfinished, still evolving contemporary reality (the openended present)." Because, according to Bakhtin, different genres and their discourses speak for certain ways of perceiving reality, for various social and cultural ideologies, this sort of playing with genres and forms, especially with the degree of irony and satire characterizing

---

26. Patricia Yaeger, *Honey-Mad Women: Emancipatory Strategies in Women's Writing* (New York, 1988), 183.

Orlando and *The Robber Bridegroom,* constitutes "a criticism (from the novel's point of view) of other genres and of the relationship these genres bear to reality." The novel, contends Bakhtin, is "a genre that is both critical and self-critical."[27]

Two primary genres brought under the novel's critical eye in *Orlando* are biography and history. In *The Robber Bridegroom,* the critique of history takes center stage. History and biography, traditionally masculine genres, are dedicated to chronicling and often celebrating masculine achievements, whether they be the achievements of a nation or an individual. In the essay "Women and Fiction," Woolf remarks that "very little is known about women. The history of England is the history of the male line, not of the female" (*CE,* II, 141). Furthermore, history and biography traditionally presume linear causality and positive progress. Both Woolf and Welty use comedy and fantasy, myth and fairy tale, to disrupt and undercut the didacticism of history and biography in order to pose questions about the role of the imagination in these extraliterary genres. At the same time, the juxtaposition with history and biography undercuts what Marilyn Arnold calls "the pat-answer world of the fairy tale."[28] The novels *novelize* history in order to recreate it from a feminist perspective. This reconstruction moves toward redefining not only history and biography but also the novel itself.

Orlando spans the history of England from the Elizabethan age up to the present—"the twelfth stroke of midnight, Thursday, the eleventh of October, Nineteen Hundred and Twenty-eight" (*O,* 329), the year of the novel's publication. Woolf's conclusion brings her fiction into contact with the present moment, with "unfinished, still evolving contemporary reality,"[29] blurring the division between imaginary and real worlds, between fiction and history. Blurring the boundaries even further, Woolf peoples her novel with historical figures: Queen Elizabeth, Nick Greene, Nell Gwynne, King Charles II, Addison, Pope, and Swift, to name just a few. But these figures are first fictionalized, then scrutinized by the

27. Bakhtin, *The Dialogic Imagination,* 7, 10.
28. Arnold, "Eudora Welty's Parody," in *Critical Essays on Eudora Welty,* ed. Turner and Harding, 34.
29. Bakhtin, *The Dialogic Imagination,* 7.

main character, Orlando. The power of approval or disapproval lies in the judgment of a fictional character.

History's linear progression is qualified by Woolf's iconoclastic hero/heroine, whose constantly developing identity over the centuries and continuing preoccupation with a single poetic-fictional work encompasses history's linear progression within a mythic perspective of return and renewal. Complicating matters further, the historical ages are experienced by and even identified with this same character who changes from male to female less than halfway through the novel. Thus from the late seventeenth century onward, Woolf presents the history of England from a woman's view, which cannot help but be a revisionist perspective. The novel thereby mocks the patriarchal assumptions of traditional historical discourse. As Howard Harper argues, the novel's opening with Orlando "slicing at the head of a Moor which swung from the rafters" (O, 13) is an image that "alludes to the system of 'masculine' values which has always made wars possible, and which has encouraged such adolescent fantasies of heroism as the one which the young Orlando is enacting here. 'He' aspires toward the same kinds of achievements that his father and grandfather did—not a very bright prospect for Orlando or 'his' culture." As the novel traces the process of Orlando's and England's maturation, themes of masculine aggression, war, and death are replaced, argues Harper, by "a more mature perception of death as inevitable in, and inseparable from, life." [30] By the final chapter, history's preoccupation with paternity and heritage, with the past, is replaced by a maternal concern with the present and future.

As a chronological account of the life of a single character, *Orlando* does abide by one of the conventions of biography; its subtitle, "A Biography," claims that generic identity. But as early as the second paragraph the narrator begins a commentary on the difficulties of a biographer's task. *Orlando* is obviously no ordinary biography. Fantasy, especially Orlando's change of gender, disrupts the ostensible biography. DiBattista's comment on this disruption is illuminating: "Woolf punctures the representational fabric of her 'objective' biography, creating a 'hole' through

---

30. Howard Harper, *Between Language and Silence: The Novels of Virginia Woolf* (Baton Rouge, 1982), 177–78, 200.

which enters a new Orlando, transformed into a woman. She then proceeds to mend or cover the gap that separates the masculine from the
feminine part of her fiction by having her biographer admit that 'often
it has been necessary to speculate, to surmise, and even to make use of
the imagination.'"[31] This puncturing of biography's conventions reveals
the assumptions underlying those conventions. Mocking the biographer's
undertaking in the asides of her narrator-biographer, Woolf questions the
assumption that an individual can be known through the description of
events and activities, through the aggregation of documents and data. As
we saw earlier, identity in *Orlando* is multifaceted and therefore cannot
be captured, summed up by the biographer's traditional methods. Woolf's
biographer makes this complaint:

> Orlando sat so still that you could have heard a pin drop. Would, indeed,
> that a pin had dropped! That would have been life of a kind. Or if a butterfly
> had fluttered through the window and settled on her chair, one could write
> about that. Or suppose she had got up and killed a wasp. Then, at once, we
> could out with our pens and write. For there would be blood shed, if only
> the blood of a wasp. And if killing a wasp is the merest trifle compared with
> killing a man, still it is a fitter subject for novelist or biographer than this
> mere wool-gathering; this thinking; this sitting in a chair day in, day out,
> with a cigarette and a sheet of paper and a pen and an ink pot. (*O,* 267)

This demand for violent action makes visible the masculine bias of traditional biography that Woolf rejects. Woolf's satire highlights in order
to deconstruct the masculine/feminine, active/passive hierarchies that
bolster the traditional biographer's art. In an essay entitled "The New
Biography," Woolf comments that life no longer "consists in action only
or in works. It consists in personality" (*CE,* IV, 230). And if personality
is multifaceted and fluid, constructed rather than inherent, then the strategies of traditional biographical discourse, whose goal is to represent a
fixed and unified individual personality, are likely to be inadequate. In
this same essay, Woolf elaborates on the problems facing the biographer:

---

31. DiBattista, *The Fables of Anon,* 118.

"The aim of biography," said Sir Sidney Lee, who had perhaps read and written more lives than any man of his time, "is the truthful transmission of personality," and no single sentence could more neatly split up into two parts the whole problem of biography as it presents itself to us today. On the one hand there is truth; on the other there is personality. And if we think of truth as something of granite-like solidity and of personality as something of rain-bow-like intangibility and reflect that the aim of biography is to weld these two into a seamless whole, we shall admit that the problem is a stiff one and that we need not wonder if biographers have for the most part failed to solve it. (CE, IV, 229)

The problems described in this passage are those Woolf playfully raises and solves in her fictional biography, Orlando.

Guiguet comments on Woolf's mockery of the conventions of bi-ography: "Considering that Virginia Woolf believes neither in the con-tinuity of a story, nor in the unity of a personality circumscribed in space and time, a postulate essential to the biographer, there is nothing sur-prising about her mockery." [32] But the ultimate irony of Orlando is that it is a biography—a biography of Virginia Woolf's intimate friend, Vita Sackville-West. Numerous commentators have documented the parallels between the character Orlando and Vita. Although they present a strong case for identifying Vita with Woolf's protagonist, it remains obvious that the way in which Orlando is a biography violates all the conventions of that genre. Virginia Woolf has not attempted to convey accurately the external detail, the events and achievements, of her subject's life. Rather, she concentrates her efforts on portraying the "rainbow-like intangibil-ity" (CE, IV, 229) of her friend. Woolf seeks to convey to her readers what she describes in "The New Biography" as "that queer amalgama-tion of dream and reality, that perpetual marriage of granite and rainbow" (CE, IV, 235).

Eudora Welty "feminizes" American frontier history in a similar man-ner, parodying and undercutting the assumptions and conventions im-plicit in most historical discourse about the age through her mixing of genres and her transgression of the traditional boundaries of fiction.

---

32. Guiguet, Virginia Woolf and Her Works, 269.

Many of the places, events, and characters of *The Robber Bridegroom* step straight out of Mississippi history. Historical figures like Little Harp mix easily with imagined and fairy-tale characters. In "Fairy Tale of the Natchez Trace," Welty explains that "in *The Robber Bridegroom,* the elements of wilderness and pioneer settlements, flatboats and river trade, the Natchez Trace and all its life, including the Indians and the bandits, are all to come together. The story is laid in an actual place, traces of which still exist, and in historical times" (*E,* 302). Welty cautions, however, that *The Robber Bridegroom* is no traditional historical novel (*E,* 302). Speaking before the Mississippi Historical Society, Welty remarks that the interplay of fantasy and history in *The Robber Bridegroom* was not a matter of chance: "I think it's become clear that it was by no accident that I made our local history and the legend and the fairy tale into working equivalents in the story I came to write. It was my firm intention to bind them together" (*E,* 305). Like Woolf, Welty uses the mixture of genres to call into question certain assumptions of history, in this case the frontier optimism and masculine values of America's westward expansion.

Danièle Pitavy-Souques observes that Welty likes "to explore the border line situations, the reversals, shifts and crossings of borders."[33] The American frontier is one such liminal situation, the borderline between civilization and wilderness, between order and chaos. It is a setting in process, unfixed and mutable. As such, the frontier gives lie to the belief that a cultural order is fixed, absolute, and ahistorical. It offers the ideal setting for a self-conscious exploration of the construction of cultural narratives, identities, and values.

Fairy tales, argues Barbara Harrell Carson, are "grounded on the child's need for simplicity." In a similar vein, Arnold suggests that Welty's book parodies fairy tales to make the point that "we as readers and writers must mature beyond the simplistic, if tantalizing, life-view presented in fairy tales."[34] Welty's yoking of fairy tale and history suggests that many

33. Daniele Pitavy-Souques, "A Blazing Butterfly: The Modernity of Eudora Welty," in *Welty,* ed. Devlin, 119.

34. Barbara Harrell Carson, "Eudora Welty's Dance with Darkness: *The Robber Bridegroom,*" *Southern Literary Journal,* XX (1988), 52; Arnold, "Eudora Welty's Parody," in *Critical Essays on Eudora Welty,* ed. Turner and Harding, 33.

of our historical accounts and perspectives are motivated by an equally strong drive on the part of adults and nations toward simplicity, a tantalizing desire to control flux and reduce complexity to unity. Frontier optimism was based upon a belief in the unlimited good of progress and opportunity. But the dark side of this national enthusiasm included violence and brutality often justified by a linear, progressive view of history and destiny.[35] As Michael Kreyling comments, "Extinction and fear are as much a part of *The Robber Bridegroom* as the cartoons, the borrowings from Grimm, and the frontier folklore. In this theme, violence as an indispensable part of the pioneering enterprise plays an essential part." [36]

The entry of fairy tale, myth, and legend into the realm of history emphasizes this dark side. Commenting on the similarity between the violence of fairy tales and the violence of this period in history, Welty says, "Actually, the fairy tale exceeds my story in horror. But even so, it isn't so much worse than what really went on during those frontier times, is it? History tells us worse things than fairy tales do. People were scalped. Babies had their brains dashed out against tree trunks or were thrown into boiling oil when the Indians made their captures. Slavery was the order on the plantations. The Natchez Trace outlaws eviscerated their victims and rolled their bodies downhill, filled with stones, into the Mississippi River. War, bloodshed, massacre were all part of the times" (*E*, 309).

Little Harp's rape and murder of the Indian woman, discussed earlier in this chapter, come directly from a fairy tale—the Grimms' "The Robber Bridegroom," and is an example of such fairy-tale violence. Though it derives from a fairy tale, the realistic description of brutality in this scene stands in sharp contrast to the comic tone of earlier violent scenes, such as Mike Fink's fight with Jamie Lockhart. The novel's abrupt shifts from fantasy to realism cast doubt upon its generic identity, suggesting that history itself is composed of imagination and fantasy as well as fact.

35. See Lisa K. Miller, "The Dark Side of Our Frontier Heritage: Eudora Welty's Use of the Turner Thesis in *The Robber Bridegroom*," *Notes on Mississippi Writers*, XIV (1981), 24. Miller examines Welty's treatment of frontier optimism, arguing that "like Turner, Welty celebrates our frontier experience and the freedom it symbolizes, but she also admits that the frontier fostered some rather undesirable traits as well."

36. Kreyling, *Eudora Welty's Achievement of Order*, 39.

Welty's incorporation of this gruesome fairy tale reveals the violent subtext of history's masculine bias for action, and the fate of the Indian
woman illustrates the victimization many suffered in the name of national
progress. Welty has noted that fantasy has its own "validity" and "springs
from . . . truth about human beings" (E, 311). The validity of fantasy
and the validity of history contradict and complement each other. Together, they offer a fuller, more complex portrait of a time and a spirit.

Welty makes significant changes in the fairy tale when she incorporates it into *The Robber Bridegroom* in order to dramatize anew the violence of the westward expansion and the paradoxical loss at the heart of
progress, an important theme in American literature from James Feni-
more Cooper's novels to William Faulkner's "The Bear." Welty splits the
robber bridegroom of the title into two characters: Jamie Lockhart and
Little Harp. If Jamie's confidence in himself as a hero and his too-easy
transformation from bandit to merchant denote frontier optimism and
belief in the future, Little Harp carries the burden of the period's dark
side. In their first meeting, Little Harp recognizes Jamie Lockhart as both
bandit and gentleman, saying: "Your name is Jamie Lockhart and you are
the bandit in the woods, for you have your two faces on together and I
see you both" (RB, 112). The connection between the two characters is
underscored by Lockhart's inability to kill Little Harp in this first meeting: "He half pulled out his little dirk to kill the Little Harp then and
there. But his little dirk, not unstained with blood, held back and would
not touch the feeble creature. Something seemed to speak to Jamie that
said, 'This is to be your burden, and so you might as well take it.' So he
put the little dirk back and contented himself with one more blow with
his arm, to knock the Little Harp's wind out for an hour or so" (RB,
112–13). Though Jamie Lockhart eventually kills Little Harp, Clement
Musgrove knows that Little Harp's death does not remove evil from the
world. "The time of cunning has come," he says (RB, 142).

Images of violence and annihilation in *The Robber Bridegroom* undercut
the idea of linear progress, just as Clement Musgrove's awareness of
change and death undercuts Jamie Lockhart's optimism about the future.
Some of the historical references themselves belie the period's optimism.
Welty chose a setting for *The Robber Bridegroom* that qualifies historic
optimism: the town of Rodney no longer exists because the Mississippi

River changed its course and left the town stranded inland. Albert J. Devlin notes that "in 1930 the town of Rodney, as well as China Grove, was designated 'extinct' by Mississippi's official *Guide to the Magnolia State.*" [37] By setting *The Robber Bridegroom* in a town that is officially extinct, Welty implies that progress is not always favorable, that the future can hold regression and endings just as easily as it can hold promise and beginnings.

The fate of the Natchez Indians who appear in *The Robber Bridegroom* further undermines frontier optimism. In "Some Notes on River Country," Welty describes the end of the Natchez tribe: "Their own sacrifices were great among them. When Iberville came, the Natchez had diminished to twelve hundred. They laid it to the fact that the fire had once been allowed to go out and that a profane fire burned now in its place. Perhaps they had prescience of their end—the only bit of their history that we really know" (*E,* 295). The Natchez Indians are thus an emblem of annihilation, a reminder of endings as well as violence. Early in the novel Clement connects the Indians' violence with their awareness of their demise: "The Indians know their time has come. . . . They are sure of the future growing smaller always, and that lets them be infinitely gay and cruel" (*RB,* 21). Toward the novel's end, Clement sees the Indians' fate as a pattern that all others will follow: "The savages have only come the sooner to their end; we will come to ours too. Why have I built my house, and added to it? The planter will go after the hunter, and the merchant after the planter, all having their day" (*RB,* 161). These repeated beginnings and endings form a pattern in *The Robber Bridegroom* that runs counter to traditional history's linear progression.

Through incorporating fairy tale and myth, Eudora Welty locates this particular episode of history within the context of larger, archetypal patterns. Lisa Miller notes that the "circle is a dominant image in the book." [38] Repeated circle images in *The Robber Bridegroom* offer a cyclical alternative to a progressive, linear view of history, and these circles are often associated with the Indians. During his first capture by the Indians,

37. Albert J. Devlin, "Eudora Welty's Mississippi," in *Critical Essays,* ed. Prenshaw, 170. See also Mary Hughes Brookhart and Suzanne Marrs, "More Notes on River Country," in *Welty,* ed. Devlin, 82–95.

38. Miller, "The Dark Side of Our Frontier Heritage," 21.

Clement and his friends "were encircled" and "had to go whirling and dizzied in a dance we had never suspected lay in our limbs" (RB, 22). Just before the Indians capture Jamie Lockhart, he is described as the center of a circle; the other characters "all turned like the spokes of the wheel toward this dreaming hub" (RB, 147). Clement's speech immediately preceding his capture is filled with circles and repetitions: "In the sky is the perpetual wheel of buzzards. A circle of bandits counts out the gold, with bending shoulders more slaves mount the block and go down, a planter makes a gesture of abundance with his whip, a flatboatman falls back from the tavern door to the river below with scarcely time for a splash, a rope descends from a tree and curls into a noose. And all around again are the Indians" (RB, 143–44). The novel's form is circular as well, beginning as Clement disembarks from a ship from New Orleans and ending as he boards a ship to leave New Orleans.

Using myth and fairy tale to qualify and undercut the conventions and assumptions of traditional history, Eudora Welty works not only to revise history but also to extend the province of the novel. As she says, "I think I've proved my claim that mine was not a *historical* historical novel. *The Robber Bridegroom*, from the start, took another direction: instead of burying itself deep in historical fact, it flew up, like a cuckoo, and alighted in the borrowed nest of fantasy" (E, 311).

Both *Orlando* and *The Robber Bridegroom* are novels about history, myth, fairy tale, and fantasy, novels about the plots we live by, about the stories we tell ourselves and how they affect our lives. The authors' play with the boundaries of the novel form part of the novel's development as a genre. Bakhtin reminds us that "after all, the boundaries between fiction and nonfiction, between literature and nonliterature and so forth are not laid up in heaven. Every specific situation is historical. And the growth of literature is not merely development and change within the fixed boundaries of any given definition; the boundaries themselves are constantly changing."[39] Welty makes a similar comment specifically about *The Robber Bridegroom*: "The line between history and fairy tale is not always clear, as *The Robber Bridegroom* along the way points out. And it was not from the two elements taken alone but from their interplay that

---

39. Bakhtin, *The Dialogic Imagination*, 33.

my story, as I hope, takes on its own headlong life" (*E*, 309). Virginia Woolf's *Orlando* offers a model of this sort of complex interplay. These, then, are novels not just about identity but about the identity of the novel itself, with its roots in legend, myth, and folklore, and about the novel's inclusive rather than exclusive nature—not wholly one thing or the other, not reductive and static, but various and always changing.

We must not lose sight of the fact that for all the violence of *The Robber Bridegroom* and the enormous task of rewriting culture that both texts undertake, these are comic works whose energy is fueled by humor as well as revolution. In fact, revolution is funny, and comedy is revolutionary, in *The Robber Bridegroom* and *Orlando*. Welty's comment on the rejection of *The Robber Bridegroom* by *Ladies Home Journal* in 1941 shows her awareness of the novel's revolutionary humor: "When I think of my Robber in the LHJ I laugh because I'm afraid he will have eaten all the desserts and menus, stripped all the fashion models, and all the men in the illustrations for the other stories will be tied up at least, and all the girls will be looking mussed and cross by the time the magazine is on the stands. You can tell how modest I feel about his powers [February 26, 1941]." In "The Laugh of the Medusa," Hélène Cixous associates this sort of open-ended, revolutionary perspective with women, using language wonderfully appropriate to a discussion of *The Robber Bridegroom:* "It's no accident: women take after birds and robbers just as robbers take after women and birds. They go by, fly the coop, take pleasure in jumbling the order of space, in disorienting it, in changing around the furniture, dislocating things and values, breaking them all up, emptying structures, and turning propriety upside down." [40] Welty's "borrowed nest of fantasy" becomes a site of feminine play, of challenges to the narrative traditions that marginalize women and forbid them to tell their own stories. In *Orlando* and *The Robber Bridegroom*, Virginia Woolf and Eudora Welty change around the furniture of the novel, dislocate the values of biography, history, and fairy tale, and violate their readers' expectations on every page in their exuberant transformations of traditional structures.

40. Kreyling, *Author and Agent*, 66; Cixous, "The Laugh of the Medusa," in *New French Feminisms*, ed. Marks and de Courtivron, 258.

FEMININE EPICS
Losing Battles and The Waves

I N "Mirrors for Reality," her review of Virginia Woolf's *"A Haunted House" and Other Short Stories,* Eudora Welty remarks upon particular qualities of Woolf's fiction, qualities that are central to her own writing as well. One such quality is the play of light and shadow in Woolf's work: "The impressionist dictum that light is the most important actor in the picture can also apply to the work of Virginia Woolf—here light does move often as a character and for its own sake from scene to scene and only itself remains unaffected by passion. In 'The Searchlight,' in this book, light is a character, the main character. But also it must be observed that in her stories the beam of light is manipulated; it is like a wand, it touches from here to there with the undeviating purpose of illuminating the particular in the abstract world." [1]

Nowhere in Virginia Woolf's fiction does light play as significant a role as in her novel *The Waves,* in which the interrelationships among the novel's six characters are punctuated by interludes tracing the sun's journey across the sky in the course of a single day. And nowhere in Welty's fiction is light as important as it is in *Losing Battles,* in which the movement of the sun throughout the reunion day frames the human activities within the natural world. [2]

1. Eudora Welty, "Mirrors for Reality," *New York Times Book Review,* April 16, 1944, p. 3.
2. See Larry J. Reynolds, "Enlightening Darkness: Theme and Structure in Eudora Welty's *Losing Battles,*" in *Critical Essays on Eudora Welty,* ed. Turner and Harding, 219.

The Waves begins with the creation of the day out of darkness:

The sun had not yet risen. The sea was indistinguishable from the sky, except that the sea was slightly creased as if a cloth had wrinkles in it. Gradually as the sky whitened a dark line lay on the horizon dividing the sea from the sky and the grey cloth became barred with thick strokes moving, one after another, beneath the surface, following each other, pursuing each other, perpetually. . . .

The light struck upon the trees in the garden, making one leaf transparent and then another. One bird chirped high up; there was a pause; another chirped lower down. The sun sharpened the walls of the house, and rested like the tip of a fan upon a white blind and made a blue fingerprint of shadow under the leaf by the bedroom window. The blind stirred slightly, but all within was dim and unsubstantial. The birds sang their blank melody outside. (*W,* 7–8)

Losing Battles opens with a strikingly similar lyrical evocation of the day's creation as dawn softly erodes the night's undifferentiated world, slowly illuminating and individuating the features of the landscape. Like Woolf, Welty uses domestic similes to create the scene:

When the rooster crowed, the moon had still not left the world but was going down on flushed cheek, one day short of the full. A long thin cloud crossed it slowly, drawing itself out like a name being called. The air changed, as if a mile or so away a wooden door had swung open, and a smell, more of warmth than wet, from a river at low stage, moved upward into the clay hills that stood in darkness. . . .

The distant point of the ridge, like the tongue of a calf, put its red lick on the sky. Mists, voids, patches of woods and naked clay, flickered like live ashes, pink and blue. A mirror that hung within the porch on the house wall began to flicker as at the striking of kitchen matches. Suddenly two chinaberry trees at the foot of the yard lit up, like roosters astrut with golden tails. Caterpillar nets shone in the pecan tree. A swollen shadow bulked underneath it, familiar in shape as Noah's Ark—a school bus. (*LB,* 9–10)

These are surprisingly similar openings for two novels that may seem at first glance to be worlds apart. The energetic, noisy, comic action of

Losing Battles' poor Mississippi family seems a far cry from the subdued, formal tone and sophisticated characters of *The Waves,* stripped, as it is, of plot in the traditional sense. But reading *Losing Battles* as an imaginative response to *The Waves,* as part of Eudora Welty's ongoing dialogue with the fiction of Virginia Woolf, highlights elements of Welty's artistic achievement in *Losing Battles* that a focus on the comic action can obscure.[3]

Speaking of the artistic form she sought for *The Waves,* Virginia Woolf compares the novel with poetry:

> The idea has come to me that what I want now to do is to saturate every atom. I mean to eliminate all waste, deadness, superfluity: to give the moment whole; whatever it includes. Say that the moment is a combination of thought; sensation; the voice of the sea. Waste, deadness, come from the inclusion of things that don't belong to the moment; this appalling narrative business of the realist: getting on from lunch to dinner: it is false, unreal, merely conventional. Why admit anything to literature that is not poetry— by which I mean saturated? Is that not my grudge against novelists? that they select nothing? The poets succeeding by simplifying: practically everything is left out. I want to put everything in: yet to saturate. That is what I want to do in *The Moths.*[4] It must include nonsense, fact, sordidity: but made transparent. (*WD,* 136)

Woolf achieves this paradoxical transparency and saturation by purposefully minimizing physical setting and activity in *The Waves* and foregrounding the inner worlds—worlds of emotional response and psychological perception—of her characters. She conveys these inner worlds through image, metaphor, and simile. For example, as Neville awaits the arrival of Percival, whom he loves, the physical setting of the restaurant exists merely as a representation of his anxiety and anticipation: "Already

---

3. Louise Y. Gossett, "Eudora Welty's New Novel: The Comedy of Loss," in *Critical Essays on Eudora Welty,* ed. Turner and Harding, 196. Gossett mentions *Losing Battles'* affinity with Woolf's fiction, stating that "like Virginia Woolf, [Welty] records the emergence of experience; the relationship of persons generates the fabric of life." Gossett does not, however, go on to draw any specific parallels.

4. *The Moths* was Virginia Woolf's early working title for *The Waves.*

the room, with its swing-doors, its tables heaped with fruit, with cold
joints, wears the wavering, unreal appearance of a place where one waits
expecting something to happen. Things quiver as if not yet in being.
The blankness of the white table-cloth glares" (*W,* 118). Similarly, the
petals that Rhoda floats in a basin of water create an image that recurs
throughout the novel to suggest her fragility and timidity. Rather than
tying the novel to a particular physical setting, images of the natural world
draw the novel into the extended world of human emotion and thought.
The piling up of images necessary for saturation gives the prose of *The
Waves* an extremely dense texture that *Losing Battles* shares.

Certainly *Losing Battles* includes plenty of the "appalling narrative
business" of getting from breakfast to lunch to dinner and back to breakfast again, as meals punctuate the Beecham–Renfro family's collaborative
narrative. Yet Eudora Welty specifically chose for her subject matter a
setting she could reduce as much as possible to the people themselves.
As she explains, "I wanted a clear stage to bring on this family, to show
them when they had really no props to their lives, had only themselves,
plus an indomitable will to live even with losing battles of poverty, of
any other kind of troubles, family troubles and disasters. I wanted to take
away everything and show them naked as human beings. So that fixed
the time and place" (*C,* 50). Welty's comment on her choice of the time
and place for *Losing Battles* is strikingly similar to her comments about
choosing the setting for *Delta Wedding.* In each case, Welty chooses a
setting that allows her to foreground the psychological and emotional
worlds of her characters. The two worlds could not, however, be less
alike. The abundance of Shellmound and the surrounding Delta of the
early twenties contrasts sharply with the barren, Depression-era Mississippi hills of *Losing Battles.* Whereas in *Delta Wedding* she wanted to explore her characters without the interference of disaster and hardship, in
Losing Battles she examines what hardship does to the human spirit.

Having thus reduced the context of *Losing Battles,* Welty proceeds to
"saturate" her prose through image, simile, metaphor—the very strategies that Virginia Woolf adopts for her poetic vision in *The Waves.* Paradoxically, Welty's densely textured prose serves to broaden the context of
her novel's setting beyond the confines of rural Mississippi. The hardships
of her rural Mississippi family form the particulars of the abstract worlds

of poverty and kinship she explores in this novel. When the harsh lights come on to illuminate the reunion after nightfall, a series of images evokes the abstract human destiny in which the family participates: "Suddenly the moonlit world was doused; lights hard as pickaxe blows drove down from every ceiling and the roof of the passage, cutting the house and all in it away, leaving them an island now on black earth, afloat in night, and nowhere, with only each other. In that first moment every face, white-lit but with its caves of mouth and eyes opened wide, black with the lonesomeness and hilarity of survival, showed its kinship to Uncle Nathan's, the face that floated over theirs" (*LB*, 300).

The result in each novel is the sort of "density of surface" Louis D. Rubin, Jr., describes in "Everything Brought Out in the Open: Eudora Welty's *Losing Battles*." His description of Welty's novel applies equally well to Woolf's: "It hasn't an opaque surface that hides the story and the meaning behind a texture of dense language and obscure reference. Everything is out on the surface, but the art is the surface, and every inch of the surface must be inspected."[5]

The surface in each novel is, of course, composed of language. Both *The Waves* and *Losing Battles* are novels about language and speech. Whereas Virginia Woolf's novel seeks to articulate and dramatize internal monologue and dialogue, Eudora Welty's consists almost altogether of external monologue and dialogue. As she revised *The Waves*, Virginia Woolf recorded in her diary that the novel was "resolving itself . . . into a series of dramatic soliloquies" (*WD*, 156), and she wondered how to end "save by a tremendous discussion, in which every life shall have its voice—a mosaic" (*WD*, 153). Although Woolf subsumed those voices into the single voice of Bernard, the character in the novel who is himself a novelist, that "tremendous discussion" giving a voice to each life is what Welty sought and achieved in *Losing Battles*. Speaking of this novel in a 1970 interview with Walter Clemons, Welty says that she chose the novel's setting and characters because of their affinity for the spoken word: "I needed that region, that kind of country family, because I wanted that chorus of voices, everybody talking and carrying on at once.

5. Louis D. Rubin, Jr., "Everything Brought Out in the Open: Eudora Welty's *Losing Battles*," *Hollins Critic*, VII (Spring, 1970), 3.

I wanted to try something completely vocal and dramatized" (*C*, 31). In a 1972 interview with Charles Bunting, Welty expands upon this idea: "I wanted it all to be shown forth, brought forth, the way things are in a play, have it become a novel in the mind of the reader, I mean, understood in the mind of the reader. The thought, the feeling that is internal is shown as external" (*C*, 46).

Whereas *The Waves* incorporates the external world into the characters' internal reality, *Losing Battles* takes that sort of internal reality and presents it externally. In each case, the result is the same: the novel's world exists in the language, the varied voices, of the characters.

NOVELIZED EPIC

Welty's comparison of her novel to a play raises the question of genre, a topic over which, once again, critics of *The Waves* and *Losing Battles* debate, as they did with *Orlando* and *The Robber Bridegroom*. Virginia Woolf referred to her own novel as a "very serious, mystical poetical work" (*WD*, 104). Jean Guiguet begins his discussion of *The Waves* with an attempt to define its genre. He compares it to a play, a ballet, an opera, and a poem, finally settling on the phrase "play poem." Maria DiBattista applies the terms *epic, romance,* and *heroic elegy,* finally adopting "comic romance in prose" as a descriptive title. Mary Anne Ferguson argues that "*Losing Battles* has been underestimated primarily because of indecision about its genre." Her summary of the generic labels applied to Welty's novel includes a "six-act grand old opry," "a melancholy idyll," "a bucolic ballad," and a combination of a "folk tale, a metaphor, and a realistic novel." Using Northrop Frye's terminology, Ferguson ultimately suggests that *Losing Battles* be seen as "a satiric or ironic epic."[6]

Epic is a common term in these two genre lists, and each novel carries significant epic associations. Both Woolf and Welty refer, though obliquely, to epics in relation to their respective works. Writing in her diary about the narrative voice of *The Waves,* Woolf refers to the heroines

6. Guiguet, *Virginia Woolf and Her Works,* 302; DiBattista, *The Fables of Anon,* 189; Mary Anne Ferguson, "*Losing Battles* as a Comic Epic in Prose," in *Critical Essays,* ed. Prenshaw, 305–06.

of two major epics, asking, "But who is she? I am very anxious that she should have no name. I don't want a Lavinia or a Penelope: I want 'she'" (*WD*, 140). And Welty, when told that *Losing Battles* reminded a reader of *The Iliad,* responded, "*Everything* reminds me of *The Iliad*" (*C*, 68). (Certainly Welty's use of similes in *Losing Battles* comes close to rivaling Homer's.) Both writers stress the importance of the epic theme of battle, struggle, and human effort in their works. Woolf comments, "This is also to show that the theme effort, effort dominates: not the waves: and personality: and defiance" (*WD*, 159). Welty says she wanted to show "indomitability" (*C*, 48), while the title itself points to the importance of battles, although we may more typically think of epics in terms of battles won. Finally, each novel centers upon a quest theme. The name Percival in *The Waves* calls to mind an archetypal quester; Woolf's Percival stands at the center of the other characters' search for wholeness. Classical questers are called to mind in *Losing Battles* by the names of Julia *Percival* Mortimer and *Homer* Champion. After completing his escape from prison a day early and journeying home for the reunion, Jack Renfro embarks on two more quests, first to derail and then to rescue Judge Moody's car. He is the family's hero, their Odysseus returned home, and they proudly spin out legends about his triumphs and defeats. But Jack is not the only quester in the novel. *Losing Battles* suggests, like *The Waves,* that questing is an essential human condition: The first words of Lady May Renfro, Jack Renfro's daughter, are, "What you huntin', man?" (*LB*, 353); Miss Julia Percival Mortimer's last words ask, "What was the trip for?" (*LB*, 233).

Several commentators have noted the epic qualities of *Losing Battles*. Mary Anne Ferguson identifies several epic features of the novel, including "direct speeches by the characters" and "a hero who, though not eponymous, represents the aspirations of his people." Ruth Vande Kieft describes the battle between Jack and Curly as "laced with comic 'romance,' even 'chivalry,' as the knight protects his sister's honor." Barbara Harrell Carson calls the novel a "mock heroic" and a comic evocation of *The Waste Land,* with Jack Renfro as "the knight—or Welty's version of a comic Fisher King—returned to bring new life to the Waste Land." Ruth Weston comments that "Welty has portrayed [Jack] as a knight

errant, no doubt with great delight in the ambiguous implications of the word *errant*."[7]

But to call either work an epic would require a suppression of certain characteristics of that genre along with certain qualities of the work under examination. It is more fruitful to look at the epic genre as one of the subjects of representation in these novels in the same way that the genres of biography, history, and fairy tale become subjects in *Orlando* and *The Robber Bridegroom*. The epic world view becomes one of the languages informing each work. *The Waves* and *Losing Battles* can thus be seen as novels that incorporate epic elements in order to question, reevaluate, and reformulate the classical genre and to enrich the novel itself.

In each novel a series of oppositions builds upon this central dialogue between the epic and the novel. Supporting the epic view is the chorus of undifferentiated voices seeking to recover a lost and idealized unity and wholeness. Epic time, argues Bakhtin, is past time formed into a finished, completed circle. The novel, by contrast, is aligned with the individual seeking differentiation and with time present in all its openness and inconclusiveness. Michael Kreyling posits that "in *Losing Battles* myth and history battle for the allegiance of men's minds and lives, the timeless fights the temporal, the circle struggles against the line." Ruth Vande Kieft makes a similar point, contrasting Miss Julia's "historical commitment [to] the idea of progress, change" to "the family's mythical or archetypal mode of existence, which is cyclical and repetitive." The terms *mythical, timeless, archetypal, cyclical,* and *circle* could be associated with the epic, while *history, temporal, line, progress,* and *change* are aligned with the novel.[8]

Bakhtin's essay "Epic and Novel" offers a useful definition of the epic: "The formally constitutive feature of the epic as a genre is . . . the trans-

7. Ferguson, "*Losing Battles* as a Comic Epic in Prose," in *Critical Essays,* ed. Prenshaw, 306; Vande Kieft, *Eudora Welty* (rev. ed.), 153; Barbara Harrell Carson, *Eudora Welty: Two Pictures at Once in Her Frame* (Troy, N.Y., 1992), 118, 120; Weston, *Gothic Traditions and Narrative Techniques,* 147. See also Pollock, "On Welty's Use of Allusion," 5–7.

8. Bakhtin, *The Dialogic Imagination,* 13; Kreyling, *Eudora Welty's Achievement of Order,* 144; Vande Kieft, *Eudora Welty* (rev. ed.), 156.

ferral of a represented world into the past, and the degree to which this world participates in the past. . . . The epic, as the specific genre known to us today, has been from the beginning a poem about the past, and the authorial position immanent in the epic and constitutive for it . . . is the environment of a man speaking about a past that is to him inaccessible, the reverent point of view of a descendant." Bakhtin lists the epic's "three constitutive features": "a national epic past" or "absolute past" that is the epic's subject matter; a "national tradition" that provides the epic's source; and "an absolute epic distance" separating the world of the epic from the world of the author and audience.[9] Although not exhaustive, these three characteristics provide a starting point from which to examine Virginia Woolf's and Eudora Welty's treatment of the epic.

Bakhtin describes the epic past as a "valorized past of beginnings and peak times" that "is distanced, finished and closed like a circle."[10] In *The Waves,* the mythic Elvedon of the characters' childhood forms this sort of removed, contained past perfection. Bernard's description of his visit to Elvedon with Susan is filled with Edenic reverberations: "No one has been there. The ferns smell very strong, and there are red funguses growing beneath them. Now we wake the sleeping daws who have never seen a human form; now we tread on rotten oak apples, red with age and slippery. . . . Put your foot on this brick. Look over the wall. That is Elvedon. The lady sits between the two long windows, writing. The gardeners sweep the lawn with giant brooms. We are the first to come here. We are the discoverers of an unknown land" (*W,* 17).

As the characters mature, Elvedon increasingly represents an idealized, undifferentiated world of unity that they believe is lost to them because they have grown older. It is, in fact, a state that they never possessed fully. Even in the novel's early sections we encounter divisions and disagreements among the children. From the novel's start, Rhoda feels different, separate from the others. Sitting in the classroom and listening to the math teacher, the child Rhoda feels isolated and alone: "'Now Miss Hudson,' said Rhoda, 'has shut the book. Now the terror is beginning. Now taking her lump of chalk she draws figures, six, seven, eight, and

9. Bakhtin, *The Dialogic Imagination,* 13.
10. *Ibid.,* 19.

then a cross and then a line on the black board. What is the answer? The others look; they look with understanding. Louis writes; Susan writes; Neville writes; Jinny writes; even Bernard has now begun to write. But I cannot write. I see only figures'" (*W*, 21). Jinny and Louis' kiss tortures young Susan until she wishes to "take [her] anguish and lay it upon the roots under the beech trees" (*W*, 13). Rather than a real experience in real time, Elvedon is a myth of unity against which the adult characters measure themselves and fall short.

In *Losing Battles* this epic past exists in the stories the family tells of Banner in earlier years. Though now a land of drought and poverty, Banner was, at least in the family's epic myth, an Edenic land of plenty, as Uncle Noah Webster explains to his new wife, Cleo: "Cleo, the old place here was plum stocked with squirrel when we was boys. It was overrun with quail. And if you never saw the deer running in here, I saw 'em. It was filled—it was filled!—with every kind of good thing, this old dwelling, when me and the rest of us Beecham boys grew up here under Granny and Grandpa Vaughn's strict raising. It's got everlasting springs, a well with water as sweet as you could find in this world, and a pond and a creek both" (*LB*, 189). But, as Brother Bethune comments, "Banner is better known today for what ain't there than what is" (*LB*, 188). This epic past of fertility, abundance, and battles won—if it ever fully existed—is lost to the present and must be continuously reconstituted and reshaped in memory.

Although both novels include a form of absolute epic past, that past is not the focus of the novels as it would be of an epic in Bakhtin's definition of the genre. *The Waves* and *Losing Battles* instead study the survivors' longing for this epic past and for a sense of unity, wholeness, and fulfillment that is now inaccessible to them except intermittently and briefly through reunions. Holding hands, the Beechams and Renfros form a circle to sing "Blest Be the Tie." A few minutes later the family scatters to return to their separate homes throughout Mississippi, leaving Granny Vaughn desolate and betrayed: "When nothing of them was left out there but their dust behind them, Granny still summoned them. 'Thieves, murderers, come back,' she begged. 'Don't leave me!' Her voice cracked" (*LB*, 343).

The two reunions in *The Waves* are marked by the same movement

from temporary unity to painful separation. During the first reunion of the adult, postlapsarian characters, before Percival leaves for India, Bernard describes the six characters' momentary sense of unity and communion:

> "But here and now we are together," said Bernard. "We have come together, at a particular time, to this particular spot. We are drawn into this communion by some deep, some common emotion. Shall we call it, conveniently, 'love'? Shall we say 'love of Percival' because Percival is going to India?"
>
> "No, that is too small, too particular a name. We cannot attach the width and spread of our feelings to so small a mark. We have come together (from the North, from the South, from Susan's farm, from Louis's house of business) to make one thing, not enduring—for what endures?—but seen by many eyes simultaneously. There is a red carnation in that vase. A single flower as we sat here waiting, but now a seven-sided flower, many-petalled, red, puce, purple-shaded, stiff with silver-tinted leaves—a whole flower to which every eye brings its own contribution." (*W*, 126–27)

But moments later Louis says, "We differ, it may be too profoundly" (*W*, 127), puncturing the image of unity created by Bernard's speech. During the second reunion at Hampton Court, years after Percival's death in India, Bernard again contemplates the mystery of unity and separation, noting that their unity is now harder than ever to achieve: "It was different once. . . . Once we could break the current as we chose. How many telephone calls, how many post cards, are now needed to cut this hole through which we come together, united, at Hampton Court?" (*W*, 216)

Welty describes a reunion as "everybody remembering together" (*C*, 78). According to Bakhtin, "memory, and not knowledge" is the source of an epic. Instead of "personal experience and the free thought that grows out of it," an epic develops out of "national tradition."[11] Both *The Waves* and *Losing Battles* use a form of choral or group voice to embody this sort of national or group tradition. In Woolf's novel the characters'

11. *Ibid.*, 13.

voices are not differentiated in any conventional manner. Sharing the same memories, these voices share as well the same tone, rhythm, and texture: they sound the same. And though the characters can be distinguished from one another through the individual motifs and images that mark their speeches, they are concerned throughout the novel with the same themes and issues. In her essay "On Not Knowing Greek," Woolf described the effect she sought: "The intolerable restrictions of the drama could be loosened, however, if a means could be found by which what was general and poetic, comment, not action, could be freed without interrupting the movement of the whole. It is this that the choruses supply . . . the undifferentiated voices who sing like birds in the pauses of the wind; who can comment, or sum up, or allow the poet to speak himself or supply, by contrast, another side to his conception" (*CE*, I, 5–6). The undifferentiated voices in *The Waves* share the memory of and longing for the epic past of Elvedon and childhood and seek always, hopelessly, to recover that unity.

In *Losing Battles*, Bakhtin's "national tradition" is embodied in the voice of the reunion itself, as the chorus of voices recounting the family members' shared history merges into the single, unified voice of memory. In many cases the source of the dialogue is not identified as an individual; phrases like "several voices invited him" (*LB*, 208), "all their voices rose as one" (*LB*, 218), "came a big chorus" (*LB*, 222), and "a whole chorus cried" (*LB*, 225) run throughout the text. Robert B. Heilman calls this community voice the result of the novel's interest in "group consciousness" rather than "individual psyche." He continues, "But even with certain identifying marks that help us keep Jack and Jill or Tom and Dick apart, the individual psyche is not quite the business of the novel; individuals may have idiosyncrasies, but basically they participate in the group consciousness—the style, the attitudes, the mores, the traditions of their time and place. The men and women enact parts in the myth that orders their lives." [12] And it is a myth, a consciousness that extends beyond the individuals who participate in it. Even after the family members have

---

12. Robert B. Heilman, "*Losing Battles* and Winning the War," in *Critical Essays,* ed. Prenshaw, 291.

gone home, Vaughn Renfro hears the communal voice of the reunion
speaking on and on into the night:

> As he plodded on through the racket, it rang behind him and was ahead of
> him too. It was all-present enough to spill over into voices, as everything,
> he was ready to believe now, threatened to do, the closer he might come to
> where something might happen. The night might turn into more and more
> voices, all telling it—bragging, lying, singing, pretending, protesting, swear-
> ing everything away—but telling it. Even after people gave up each other's
> company, and said goodbye and went home, if there was only one left,
> Vaughn Renfro, the world around him was still one huge, soul-defying re-
> union. (*LB*, 349)

But neither novel permits this communal voice to occupy center stage
alone. Instead, each narrative focuses on the struggle between the undifferentiated voices lauding the past and the voice of the individual insisting on the present and future. "The Banner fold," comments Ruth
Vande Kieft, "are like one of those marvelous choruses in which each
singer is an accomplished professional, and from anywhere, at any time,
may emerge as a soloist, virtuosic, though unique in timbre and quality.
But even within the general harmony (this is comedy), dissonance and
cacophony erupt." Susan Donaldson's perceptive reading of *Losing Battles'*
opposing discourses illuminates *The Waves* as well: "*Losing Battles* is a text
not just about two different world views but two opposing modes of
discourse, that is, two different structures of representation and ways of
speaking, listening, and seeing that are socially constituted and consti-
tuting, determined and determining." [13] All the characters of *The Waves,*
but especially Louis and Rhoda, fight to resist the very unity they long
for. Bernard's golden ring becomes in Louis' speech a vise, "a chain
whirling round, round, in a steel-blue circle" (*W,* 137). Rhoda is both
drawn and repelled by reunion with the others: "I condemn you. Yet my
heart yearns towards you. I would go with you through the fires of death.

---

13. Vande Kieft, *Eudora Welty* (rev. ed.), 149; Susan Donaldson, "Contradictors,
Interferers, and Prevaricators: Opposing Modes of Discourse in Eudora Welty's *Losing
Battles,*" in *Eye of the Storyteller,* ed. Trouard, 32.

Yet am happiest alone" (*W,* 220). Although the epic unquestioningly celebrates the past and unity, in *The Waves* the epic is situated within the context of the novel's heteroglossia. Rather than celebrating the epic perspective, Woolf's novel chronicles the struggle between the need for unity and the need for self-definition and independence.[14]

In *Losing Battles* the struggle for separation and autonomy is even stronger and more central than in *The Waves.* Gloria Renfro, Miss Julia Mortimer, and Judge Moody give voice most often to the individual perspective and fight against the family's desire to subsume its separate members. Seeking to separate Jack and Lady May from the rest of the family, longing for a house of their own, Gloria asserts and reasserts her independence from the Beechams and Renfros. "Gloria, the orphan," explains Louise Y. Gossett, "is the voice of the present disclaiming the past." [15] Gloria outrages the family by claiming that she is trying to "save" Jack, to rescue him from his "mighty family." She vows, "We'll live to ourselves one day yet. . . . I'm going to take Jack and Lady May and we're going to get clear away from *everybody,* move to ourselves" (*LB,* 307). But the communal voice speaks in comic rejoinder as Jack's younger sisters, Etoyle and Elvie, cry out, "Carry me with you" (*LB,* 307).

Miss Julia Percival Mortimer, Banner's schoolteacher, viewed herself in epic terms. "She was Saint George," explains Gloria, "and Ignorance was the dragon" (*LB,* 236). Fighting throughout her life against the dragon of ignorance that binds the family members to one another and to Banner, she poses a more serious threat than Gloria to the unified voice of the reunion in her insistence that the children of Banner school should leave the area, make "something" of themselves, and "*put* Banner on the map" (*LB,* 265). Of course, from the family's perspective, Banner's boundaries mark the end of the significant world; they have no need for a place on a map of the larger world. Indeed, as Judge Moody discovers, Banner's roads are remarkably impervious to maps and thwart both in-

14. DiBattista, *The Fables of Anon,* 163. DiBattista takes a similar view of the primary struggle in the novel, arguing that "self-definition is the central problem in *The Waves*" and that "each voice laments its own condition as a threshold being." Her discussion of this struggle tends, however, to give primacy to the individual voice over the chorus.

15. Gossett, "Eudora Welty's New Novel," in *Critical Essays on Eudora Welty,* ed. Turner and Harding, 202.

siders trying to leave the community and outsiders trying to intrude. Barbara Harrell Carson points out that the map at the start of the book is not one designed to situate Banner in the larger world: "The nature of the territory Welty is exploring is suggested at the outset in the map printed before the text of the novel. . . . Shaped like a heart—not the symmetrical greeting card variety, but the real organ—with Banner Road going through it like an arrow, the map prepares the reader for Miss Beulah's declaration that Banner is 'the very heart' . . .—of Boone County (she means), but also of humankind."[16]

The other map in the novel, the one that Miss Julia Mortimer sends to Judge Moody, is similarly useless for navigation of roads, but it serves as an effective emotional guide to remind the Judge of his debt and responsibilities to his former teacher. Upon receiving in the mail an envelope containing "only a map she'd drawn me, showing how to get from Ludlow to Alliance and where she lived" (*LB*, 292–93), the Judge and his wife started out for Banner. But the map is "a maze," says Judge Moody. "Just a maze. There wasn't much right about her thinking any longer. I didn't try to go by it—but I lost my own way on Boone County roads for the first time I can remember. I could almost believe I'd been *maneuvered* here" (*LB*, 293).

As one who understands the value of maps, Miss Julia is a confirmed outsider to Banner's communal, epic perspective, though she was born and raised in nearby Ludlow. "'She wanted us to quit worshipping our-selves quite so wholeheartedly!' cried Miss Beulah" (*LB*, 228), objecting to Miss Julia's opposition to Banner's focus on itself. She stands as the representative of the individual in opposition to the group. "She never did learn how to please," Miss Beulah comments (*LB*, 282). "And she couldn't beat time when she marched us," complains Aunt Birdie. "She run ahead of us" (*LB*, 283).

Miss Julia Mortimer cannot beat time. Aged and ailing, she falls under the abusive care of Lexie Renfro. "Is this Heaven," asks Miss Julia in her letter to Judge Moody, "where you lie wide open to the mercies of others who think they know better than you what's best—what's true and what isn't? Contradictors, interferers, and prevaricators—are those angels?"

16. Carson, *Two Pictures at Once*, 119.

(*LB*, 289). The family's epic narratives do not meet Miss Julia's demand for *truth*, which depends on written evidence, not oral storytelling. "She read in the daytime" (*LB*, 283), much to the disapproval of the story-telling Banner population. Judge Moody, one of Miss Julia's early students, is another advocate of the written word. In his argument with the family over the evidence for Gloria's parentage, the two sides of the battle are clearly delineated. "I would just like a little evidence. My kind of evidence," complains the Judge. "'They've told a patched-together family story and succeeded in bringing out no more evidence than if their declared intention had been to conceal it. . . . I saw there was a postcard,' he told her. . . . 'But a postcard isn't the same evidence as a license to marry or a marriage certificate'" (*LB*, 309–10). The outraged family explodes, "It's better!" (*LB*, 310), rejecting the Judge's "kind of evidence" as thoroughly as he rejects theirs. Their postcard—a family artifact and a form of personal communication—and the stories about Sam Dale and Rachel Sojourner that the family collaborates to spin out from its brief message form, in their eyes, a far more convincing proof than any impersonal, public document could. Susan Donaldson explains: "As confirmed oral storytellers, the clan implicitly rejects the possibility of alternative forms of discourse, in particular the reading and writing that Miss Julia Mortimer so relentlessly champions. Such solitary acts suggest an openness to multiple impressions and interpretations—possibilities all too threatening to the oral chain of experience defining the family and its sense of community."[17]

The communal voice grows strongest and loudest when the family feels itself threatened by an outside, separating force. When Gloria, who is "not afraid of pencil and paper" (*LB*, 94), resists incorporation into the family, crying, "I don't want to be a Beecham!" (*LB*, 259), the family responds as a single, violent force to make Gloria acquiesce. The hands forcing watermelon down her throat are "robbed of sex" (*LB*, 259) in this sexually suggestive and violent scene: "Let's cram it down her little red lane! Let's make her say Beecham!" (*LB*, 260). The voices ordering her to "say Beecham!" (*LB*, 259) lose their individuality and merge into

---

17. Donaldson, "Contradictors, Interferers, and Prevaricators," in *Eye of the Story-teller*, ed. Trouard, 36.

a single voice, the voice of the reunion: "Somebody shouted, 'Wash it down her crook!' ... A melony hand forced warm, seed-filled hunks into Gloria's sagging mouth. 'Why, you're just in the bosom of your own family,' somebody's voice cried softly as if in condolence. Melon and fingers together went into her mouth. 'Just swallow,' said the voice. 'Everybody's got something they could cry about'" (*LB*, 260). From Gloria's individualist perspective, the family's insistence on unity and belonging is a form of violence, a metaphoric rape; from their perspective, Gloria's desire to move away from Banner is a metaphoric dismembering of the communal body.

Miss Lexie Renfro's treatment of Julia Mortimer is even more violent and violating. She brags, "I tied her up, that was the upshoot. ... Tied her in bed" (*LB*, 269). Worse, from Julia Mortimer's perspective, Lexie deprives her of the ability to write: "'In the long run, I got her pencil away from her,' said Miss Lexie, speaking faster. 'I could pull harder than she could'" (*LB*, 274). Deprived of her pencil, Miss Julia writes with a straight pin, sticking holes in the cover of her speller. Miss Lexie wants her patient to talk instead of reading and writing, but in response to her constant questions, Miss Julia replies, "Suppose you take your presence out of here. How can I read with you in the house with me?" (*LB*, 267). Throughout the battle, Miss Julia seeks to silence Lexie's incessant chatter, while the family struggles to suppress the written word.

Miss Julia Mortimer is correct when she writes, "Both sides were using the same tactics" (*LB*, 287). The tactic is language, two modes of discourse, each trying to silence the other. *Losing Battles* is a novel about the struggle of the oral, communal tradition of the epic and its view of reality against all those individual perceptions it silences and marginalizes to sustain order and unity, against the individual's desire to articulate a unique vision and assert a unique truth. Vaughn Renfro, Jack's younger brother, is the only character in the novel whose vision can encompass both sides. Welty points out that Vaughn's post-reunion meditation is the only occasion in *Losing Battles* when she "[gets] into somebody's mind." Though he is a confirmed member of the family, a part of the reunion, he is also the "best speller." He has, according to Welty, "an awareness that there [is] something over and beyond the circle of the family that

[is] still capable of being understood." [18] Significantly, he is the only family member in the novel who listens more than he talks: "He heard every sound going on, repeating itself, increasing, as if it were being recollected by loud night talking to itself" (*LB*, 349).

Rather than providing a model for the novel as epic, *The Waves* offers a model of the novelization of the epic. Both *The Waves* and *Losing Battles* represent the power and attraction of the epic world and the characters' longing to recover it, while simultaneously showing its shortcomings and impossibility. At the same time, the desire of the individual for autonomous self-definition is equally suspect. These works grow out of the tension between the epic's unity and finality and the novel's inconclusive and partial present. The unified, complete epic heros of each—Percival of *The Waves* and Sam Dale Beecham of *Losing Battles*—die and are replaced by incomplete characters—Bernard and Jack—who are still developing. Individual mortality replaces epic immortality. Bernard's final words in *The Waves* are "O Death!" (*W*, 297).

In the closing scenes of *Losing Battles*, Jack, representative of the oral, communal mode, and Gloria, letter writer and individualist, traverse a path that cuts between the epic past and individual future. Walking through the graveyard where Miss Julia Mortimer is being buried along with the epic ancestors, the young couple plans a life together that continues rather than resolves the tension between unity and individual. Gloria tells Jack that "some day yet, we'll move to ourselves. And there'll be just you and me and Lady May." To this Jack responds, "And a string of other chaps to come along behind her. . . . You just can't have too many, is the way I look at it" (*LB*, 415–16).

CONCENTRIC STRUCTURE

The central dialogue in *The Waves* and *Losing Battles* between the epic and the novel is cast in a concentric narrative form, similar to that of *To the Lighthouse* and *Delta Wedding*, underscoring the movement back and

18. Albert J. Devlin and Peggy Whitman Prenshaw, "A Conversation with Eudora Welty," in *Welty*, ed. Devlin, 15–16.

forth between group to individual. And as in *The Robber Bridegroom,* the circle is the dominant image throughout each work. *The Waves* opens with a circle in the first line: "'I see a ring,' said Bernard, 'hanging above me. It quivers and hangs in a loop of light'" (*W,* 9). Neville's first speech expands the circle into "a globe . . . hanging down in a drop against the enormous flanks of some hill" (*W,* 9). And Susan's third observation includes "a caterpillar . . . curled in a green ring" (*W,* 9). These circular images are repeated throughout the work as the circle expands to enclose the six characters. The characters become "a six-sided flower; made of six lives" (*W,* 229). Bernard, the final speaker, sums up their lives as a "globe, full of figures" (*W,* 238). Reinforcing these circular images is the important image of light discussed earlier. The circular pattern created by the interludes traces the sun's course in an arc across the sky, the circle of a single day that encloses the narratives of the six characters.

Losing Battles is filled with concentric patterns as well. Vaughn's meditation after the reunion is marked by circle images reminiscent of those in Clement Musgrove's musings; Vaughn hears "that the whole wheel of the sky made the sound as it kept letting fall the soft fire of its turning" (*LB,* 349). The reunion itself is one moment in a cyclic pattern of yearly gatherings. During the "joining-of-hands" (*LB,* 334), the family actually forms a circle, which is emblematic of the reunion's dream of epic unity. Banner's roads, as outsiders soon discover, seem to run in circles, bringing Judge Moody back to the reunion and Miss Julia Mortimer's funeral back to Banner. The day's storytelling and the adventures that land Jack in the penitentiary begin with the gold wedding ring Ella Fay takes from the family Bible, the ring that comes around again in the story of the Beechams' parents' deaths: "'And it's the ring Ella Fay carried to school that morning? Are we back around to that?' Aunt Cleo asked. 'It's the same gold ring, and all the one sad story,' Miss Beulah said, patting Granny's shoulder, smoothing out the lace collar" (*LB,* 214). Finally, Ella Fay's flirtation with Curly Stovall, the flirtation that resulted in the ring's loss, surrounds the stories of the reunion and Jack's adventures, as Ella Fay threatens to marry Curly Stovall toward the end of the novel.

Even time forms a circle of mythic, epic repetitions in *Losing Battles* as the past repeats itself in the family's view. Michael Kreyling describes Jack as a "reincarnation" of Sam Dale Beecham: "Both young men are

the apple of the family's eye. Both are taken from the circle by a foreign thing called the government, and both courted red-haired girls with mysterious pasts. The reunion insists that Jack recapitulate the abbreviated life of Sam Dale." [19] Lady May, conceived before Jack and Gloria's marriage, is proof enough for the reunion that Rachel Sojourner was Gloria's mother: "Like mother, like daughter! Isn't that the old-timey rule?" (*LB*, 253) The generational circle becomes one more strategy the reunion uses in its defense against the individual.

The speaking voices of each novel form a circle as well. At the center of each circle lies that unattainable epic past, a form of emptiness, absence, and loss; the voices of the present circle around this center and try through language to recover or recreate the epic unity. In the central section of *The Waves,* the characters meet for dinner before Percival leaves for India. In his silence, Percival represents for the other characters the unity and wholeness associated with the epic past. As Louis puts it, "It is Percival . . . sitting silent as he sat among the tickling grasses when the breeze parted the clouds and they formed again, who makes us aware that these attempts to say, 'I am this, I am that,' which we make, coming together, like separated parts of one body and soul, are false. Something has been left out from fear" (*W*, 137).

But in the next section Percival dies, and his absence forms the silent center, the symbol of lost wholeness around which the other six characters revolve. Thus loss itself generates a unity of sorts. Bernard remarks, "About him my feeling was: he sat there in the centre. Now I go to that spot no longer. The place is empty" (*W*, 153). Just as the first and last sections of *To the Lighthouse* frame the central "Time Passes" section that is emptied of all human presence, so the six characters' monologues frame the silent absence of Percival, seeking to understand and make peace with the world of human loss symbolized by his death.

Like *The Waves,* Welty's *Losing Battles* grows out of and encircles a center of loss, death, and absence. At the physical center of the novel is the story of the Beechams' parents' death, the central loss and mystery associated with the disappearance of Banner's Edenic plenty and the family's epic past. At the center of that accident is a gaping hole in the

19. Kreyling, *Eudora Welty's Achievement of Order*, 146.

Banner bridge—"The first few rows of planks had give way and fell in, or somebody had carried 'em off out of meanness, nobody ever knew" (*LB*, 210)—and a gap in the family's narrative and Welty's narrative, the mystery of the motive behind the couple's journey: "What errand was they both so bent on when they hitched and cut loose from the house so early and drove out of sight of Grandpa and Granny, children and all, that morning?" (*LB*, 213) At the center of the reunion is Grandpa Vaughn's empty seat: his death one year earlier is a point of reference for the reunion. Meanwhile, winding its way in and out and around the events and stories of the reunion is Miss Julia Mortimer's funeral.[20]

But as in *To the Lighthouse* and *Delta Wedding*, this empty center is transformed into a generative absence that gives the fiction its form and shape. Percival's absence moves the other characters toward self-definition, a state simultaneously sought after and avoided. Neville says, "Change is no longer possible. We are committed. Before, when we met in a restaurant in London with Percival, all simmered and shook; we could have been anything. We have chosen now, or sometimes it seems the choice was made for us—a pair of tongs pinched us between the shoulders. I chose. I took the print of life not outwardly, but inwardly upon the raw, the white, the unprotected fibre" (*W*, 213–14). This individual loss is ultimately a textual gain for the novel as a work of art. As DiBattista explains, "What *The Waves* forfeits in abandoning a unanimous vision, it gains in the multiplicity and diversity of its estranged figures, each projecting his various interpretations on the copious moment, the hoard of life."[21]

Carolyn Williams connects the intersection of loss and self-definition with language, with the articulation of a self in Woolf's fiction: "This interdependence of emptiness and definition . . . typifies the conundrum of *The Waves*, where life after earliest childhood becomes a perpetually more articulated sense of loss, an effort to reconfigure fragments of an identity around the memory of a 'complete body,' a body impossible ever to 'have' or to be. For as soon as any subject begins to articulate a self

20. Weston, *Gothic Traditions and Narrative Techniques*, 153, describes the various stories of *Losing Battles* as being "spun out, weblike, from the still center of a corpse."
21. DiBattista, *The Fables of Anon*, 176.

who could presume to 'have,' at that moment separation and incompleteness also establish themselves. This is the myth of identity in *The Waves*, which already in its opening chapter celebrates the simultaneity of language and loss."[22] Thus loss and emptiness become the condition for language and therefore for fiction. The monologues that constitute *The Waves* all grow out of loss and absence as the characters attempt to define and articulate their separate identities. Virginia Woolf's diaries suggest that the novel itself grew out of one of Woolf's many early encounters with loss and absence—the death of her brother Thoby:

> Here in the few minutes that remain, I must record, heaven be praised, the end of *The Waves*. I wrote the words O Death fifteen minutes ago, having reeled across the last ten pages with some moments of such intensity and intoxication that I seemed only to stumble after my own voice, or almost, after some sort of speaker (as when I was mad) I was almost afraid, remembering the voices that used to fly ahead. Anyhow, it is done; and I have been sitting here these fifteen minutes in a state of glory, and calm, and some tears, thinking of Thoby and if I could write Julian Thoby Stephen 1881–1906 on the first page. (*WD*, 165)

Woolf's words suggest that writing the novel served the same purpose for her that the gathering to remember Percival served for her characters.

Although there is no similar diary entry from Welty, the years she spent writing *Losing Battles*—1954 to 1968—were marked by personal loss. Her brother Walter died in January, 1959. Welty spent much of the next six years nursing her mother through her final illness. Her mother's death in January, 1966, was followed within days by the unexpected death of her brother Edward.[23] Death and loss surrounded her writing of the novel. And, as in *The Waves*, in *Losing Battles* absence and loss generate fiction, spinning out story after story, as the family seeks to create and re-create itself through language. Every story recounted at the reunion grows around some sort of loss: Jack's imprisonment at Parchman, Sam Dale's death in the war, Nathan's missing arm, the death of the Beecham

---

22. Williams, "Virginia Woolf's Rhetoric of Enclosure," 46.
23. Kreyling, *Author and Agent*, 191–204.

parents. As the stories tumble out over one another, the elegiac tone sometimes overcomes the comic tone. The attempt to fill empty spaces, to compensate for loss, grows desperate at times. But in *Losing Battles* the power of language is ultimately transformative, creating presence out of absence in a way that it does not in *The Waves*. Early in the novel the telling of Jack's story brings him home: "Well: you brought him" (*LB*, 75), says Miss Lexie Renfro. Later, the recounting of Jack's escape reduces Judge Moody, who could command Jack's return to prison, to helpless silence. The family's account of Miss Julia Mortimer's story recalls her from death as their telling of her story makes the former schoolteacher as vivid a character as any in the novel, though she never enters the pages alive. When Judge Moody reads the first line of her letter, "I have always pretty well known what I was doing" (*LB*, 287), the members of the reunion shout in recognition: "He might have just flashed Miss Julia's face on the screen of the bois d'arc tree with a magic lantern" (*LB*, 287). And when Lexie Renfro finishes her tragic story of Miss Julia's last months, Beulah remarks, "I can see that old schoolteacher this minute plainer than I can see you, Lexie Renfro, after your back's turned" (*LB*, 273). Julia Mortimer's funeral forms another reunion in the novel, as her absence brings her many successful pupils circling back in on Banner. Finally, through all the activity and debate, the storytelling of the central reunion keeps Granny alive, halting her occasional slips toward death and absence. If language and fiction spring from separation and loss in *Losing Battles,* they are transformed in Welty's text into successful weapons for combatting these enemies.

THE FEMININE STORYTELLER

"Perhaps Woolf entertained in her original plan for *The Waves* a feminization of the epic," says Maria DiBattista. In her analysis of *The Waves* DiBattista argues that the novel "extends Woolf's sense of feminine creativity." She notes that "at the center of Elvedon is a lady *writing*. The woman is no longer a transmitter, but an interpreter of reality."[24]

Other readers, however, question such a reading, arguing that the

24. DiBattista, *The Fables of Anon*, 148–49, 157.

view of female creativity presented in *The Waves* is ambiguous and fraught with hesitancies and ambivalence. Unlike *Orlando,* in which the artist undergoes a biological transformation from a man to a woman and in which creativity is reimaged as feminine, or *To the Lighthouse,* in which the artistic vision of a woman, Lily Briscoe, triumphs over the patriarchal constraints, in *The Waves* the artist remains housed in a masculine body throughout the novel. Bernard, the novel's creator of stories, says of himself, "But 'joined to the sensibility of a woman' (I am here quoting my own biographer) 'Bernard possessed the logical sobriety of a man'" (*W,* 76). Eileen B. Sypher objects that this model of androgyny is a traditional patriarchal construct: "This feature of representation raises questions about the legitimacy of the concept of androgyny as it reproduces the historical pattern of males absorbing the female part of the brain and not vice-versa." Jane Marcus argues that Bernard's "recurring vision 'of a lady at a table writing, the gardeners with their great brooms sweeping'" is a "patriarchal representation of Woman as Culture" and "has more to do with [Bernard's] own image as a ruling-class writer than the possibility of woman's producing culture." [25]

Howard Harper convincingly demonstrates that the language of literary creativity in *The Waves* belongs almost entirely to the male characters: "[The word *poetry*] belongs to males: it is spoken thirteen times in the book, never by a woman; *poem(s)* is spoken nineteen times by males, three by females. The uses of *novel(s)* and *story(ies)* are even more overwhelmingly male: the former word is spoken five times, always by males; the latter fifty-two times, once by a female. All of this confirms the reader's intuition that the realm of literature in *The Waves* . . . is the province of males." [26] Over and over again, the poet with whom Bernard aligns himself is Byron, for whom writing poetry was equated with constructing a masculine self.

Whereas Bernard is a creator of stories, Neville a poet and scholar, and even Louis an avid reader of poetry, the women of the novel move in traditionally female spheres of creativity. Jinny's body serves as her

---

25. Eileen B. Sypher, "*The Waves:* A Utopia of Androgyny?" in *Virginia Woolf: Centennial Essays,* ed. Elaine K. Ginsberg and Laura Moss Gottlieb (Troy, N.Y., 1983), 191; Jane Marcus, "Britannia Rules *The Waves,*" in *Virginia Woolf,* ed. Homans, 230.
26. Harper, *Between Language and Silence,* 241.

creation and her artistic medium. She says, "I can imagine nothing beyond the circle cast by my body" (W, 128–29). Susan's creativity is maternal; she bears and raises children, creates a home, and tends a garden.
Rhoda, the one woman in the novel who is not tied to a traditional
female role, commits suicide: she does not succeed in finding a nontraditional feminine form of expression. These limited representations of
feminine creativity must be weighed against the image of the woman
writing in Elvedon. Sypher offers a strongly stated summary of the problems of female creativity as portrayed in *The Waves*:

> We see in *The Waves* many traces of female creators, silenced or troubled.
> The final writer is the writer of the interludes, the "set," and the writer of
> the soliloquies. The writer is completely invisible. Every attempt has been
> made to efface any trace of reaction, any trace of summary. It would be
> difficult to claim this is an "image" of a female. The more visible, represented
> creators, on the other hand, are the males, the androgynous writer being
> one of them. Representation itself may not confer special status, but it does
> signify the greater visibility of male creators and a painful impossibility of
> the same kind of visibility for the females.[27]

The Waves, then, presents an ambivalent image of feminine creativity,
and specifically of female *authoring*. Even the image of the androgynous
artist is ambivalent. Bernard is a failure as a writer and in the novel's final
pages gives up on his book: "My book, stuffed with phrases, has dropped
to the floor. It lies under the table to be swept up by the charwoman
when she comes wearily at dawn looking for scraps of paper, old tram
tickets, and here and there a note screwed into a ball and left with
the litter to be swept up. . . . I have done with phrases" (W, 294–95). In
the end, Bernard lapses into silence, having never found the language he
needed.[28]

Welty's response, by contrast, is a celebration of feminine creativity
and authoring. *Losing Battles* consists, in great part, of women telling

27. Sypher, "A Utopia of Androgyny?" in *Centennial Essays,* ed. Ginsberg and Gottlieb, 196.

28. His failure as a writer suggests that it is a mistake to read Bernard as a mouthpiece
for Woolf's view of the writer's art, as some critics have.

stories about women. Mary Anne Ferguson comments that "perhaps the greatest innovation of the book is the extent to which we hear the voices of women telling the epic story." Ruth Vande Kieft connects storytelling in *Losing Battles* to other traditionally female art forms: "[Etoyle] is both admired and rebuked for her well-known tendency to 'embroider' a tale, the metaphor itself linking the art of narrative with another form of folk art cultivated by Banner women." Miss Beulah's voice is the loudest as she orchestrates the storytelling throughout, earning her James Boatwright's labels—"the priestess of these verbal rites" and "the arbiter of speech." Though frail-voiced Uncle Percy begins the family narrative, the voices of Gloria, of Miss Lexie, of Aunts Nanny, Birdie, and Beck, and of Miss Julia Mortimer herself (through her letter), gradually take over the storytelling. Eben E. Bass notes that both written and oral language are the province of women: "Whether through Julia's book language (meant to lead Banner beyond parochialism) or Granny Vaughn's oral history (to perpetuate family values), male authority is questioned: not out of malice or subversion, but rather in an undercurrent of irony, sometimes funny, sometimes sad." [29] In a playful reversal of silenced women, Welty's novel resounds with the voices of women, traditional and nontraditional, young and old.

In addition to dominating the telling of stories, the women are their own stories' central subjects. They narrate stories of their own struggles, quests, and endurance. Except for the opening tale of Jack's adventures—adventures that are initiated by his sister's misbehavior—the narratives about men are secondary, subplots in women's stories. The tales of Sam Dale Beecham's childhood wound and his death in the war become subplots in the story told to solve the mystery of Gloria's identity. The tale describing Nathan's crime and punishment serves to link the stories of Gloria's birth and Miss Julia Mortimer's role in the family. Judge Moody's story is subsumed into the story of Julia Mortimer's life and death. And behind all the telling lies Aunt Cleo's curiosity, her questions spurring the other women on to tell of their lives.

29. Ferguson, "*Losing Battles* as a Comic Epic in Prose," in *Critical Essays,* ed. Prenshaw, 322; Vande Kieft, *Eudora Welty* (rev. ed.), 150; James Boatwright, "Speech and Silence in *Losing Battles,*" *Shenandoah,* XXV (Spring, 1974), 8; Eben E. Bass, "The Languages of *Losing Battles,*" *Studies in American Fiction,* XXI (Spring, 1993), 67.

The female storytellers of *Losing Battles* mark a great shift from the silenced women of *Delta Wedding* and the lying and plotting women of *The Robber Bridegroom*. The women of *Losing Battles* are responsible for creating and recounting the narratives that shape their world. They compose both the epic stories and the individual narratives that battle against the epic view. Julia Mortimer calls these speakers liars; rather, they are fiction makers. Their prevarications give meaning to their lives. She is right, however, in her claim that both sides in this battle use the same tactics in a struggle neither side wins; but together, they create an artistic triumph. At the center of all this feminine storytelling sits Great-Granny Vaughn, the matriarch, hearing it all. Ultimately, the stories all tell the events of her life. But if the women are the verbal artists of *Losing Battles,* they are still artists by avocation and not by vocation. Only in her next novel, *The Optimist's Daughter*, does Eudora Welty create a female character in whom artistic avocation and vocation coincide.

ELEGIAC CARNIVALS

The Optimist's Daughter and *To the Lighthouse*

I
N her foreword to Woolf's *To the Lighthouse,* Welty explains that the process of discovery in reading is not limited to one's first reading of a creative work, but is ongoing and ever changing: "Personal discovery is the direct and, I suspect, the appropriate route to *To the Lighthouse.* Yet discovery, in the reading of a great original work, does not depend on its initial newness to us. No matter how often we begin it again, it seems to expand and expand again ahead of us. Reading *To the Lighthouse* now, I am still unwarned, still unprepared in the face of it, and my awe and my delight remain forever cloudless." It is not surprising then that Welty, in writing a novel that examines the connections among love, loss, memory, and art, a novel that uses the family as the ground for this examination, returned once again to Woolf's treatment of the same issues in *To the Lighthouse.* Michael Kreyling's analysis of *The Optimist's Daughter* in *Eudora Welty's Achievement of Order* offers the only significant discussion heretofore of the creative connections between *The Optimist's Daughter* and *To the Lighthouse.* He considers the novels' shared concern with distance, "whether the distance is created by the passing of time or by the gulf between the self and the public role, self and society, self and loved one, and self and the truth." Kreyling claims that "Laurel contends with the issues of distance in human relationships, with memory, and with faith in human life—issues that concern Virginia Woolf in *To the Lighthouse.*" The novels share as well a concern with the woman artist; Maria DiBattista's description of *To the Lighthouse* as "a novel about the libera-

tion of the poetic voice" applies equally well to *The Optimist's Daughter*.[1] Here, in what may be Welty's last novel, we find the most extensive exploration of what it means to be a woman and an artist. This exploration begins in *The Robber Bridegroom* with the lies and plots of Rosamond and Salome, and it continues with Laura McRaven's drawings in *Delta Wedding* and the oral storytelling of the Renfro–Beecham women of *Losing Battles*. In *The Optimist's Daughter*, questions about artistry and art, about art as a process of living in relation with others, and about the tensions, choices, and triumphs that await a woman artist—questions that are implicit in her earlier works—are explored in Laurel McKelva Hand's coming to terms with memory and the past.

The Optimist's Daughter reconsiders in a more mature and serious fashion many of the concerns and themes of *To the Lighthouse* so important to *Delta Wedding*. In treating the themes of love and marriage in *The Optimist's Daughter*, however, Welty discards the pastoral mode that sets the predominant tone of her earlier novel. In fact, Laurel McKelva Hand, the heroine of *The Optimist's Daughter*, must move beyond the simplistic view of marriage implied by *Delta Wedding*'s pastoral vision to an understanding of the complexity, the combination of sustenance and violence, that characterizes the fuller view of marriage that Woolf gives us in *To the Lighthouse*. Although the family provides the ground for this study of marriage and gender relationships, as it does in *To the Lighthouse* and *Delta Wedding*, in *The Optimist's Daughter* Welty narrows and intensifies her focus, reducing the family to its smallest nuclear unit: two parents and a child. Welty's first draft of the story that eventually became *The Optimist's Daughter* was titled "An Only Child,"[2] suggesting that this intensified focus on the relationship between parents and child was important to her configuration of the narrative from the start. The death of the mother, the father's remarriage and death, the marriage of the daughter, and the death of her husband provide the variations of familial and marital relationships that the novel examines.

Writing of *To the Lighthouse*, Rachel Blau DuPlessis says, "And by the

---

1. Welty, Foreword to *To the Lighthouse*, vii; Kreyling, *Eudora Welty's Achievement of Order*, 153–54; DiBattista, *The Fables of Anon*, 66.

2. Sally Wolff, "Among Those Missing: Phil Hand's Disappearance from *The Optimist's Daughter*," *Southern Literary Journal*, XXV (1992), 76.

death of Mrs. Ramsay at midbook, the affirmation of the romantic, po-
larized couple is put definitively in the past. In the third section, community and selfhood must be negotiated in the absence of çouple love
that once mediated them."[3] In a similar manner, in *The Optimist's Daughter*, the negotiation of familial and romantic relationships takes place
through a character who is both orphan and widow, suggesting that Welty
has left behind the romance narratives of her earlier novels for a new
narrative form.

The threat and loss that haunt the pastoral vision of *Delta Wedding*
become as central to *The Optimist's Daughter* as they are to *To the Lighthouse*. The novel begins with Judge McKelva's illness and unexpected
death; the first section ends with Laurel, his daughter, accompanying his
body home to Mount Salus for burial. Instead of the removed, insular
time and place of *Delta Wedding, The Optimist's Daughter* takes place in a
recognizably post-1950 Cold War world fraught by imperfections and
"blundering." The most salient feature of the world of *The Optimist's
Daughter*, like the world of "Time Passes," is change. The Second World
War intrudes in *The Optimist's Daughter* as the First World War does in
To the Lighthouse, cutting short Laurel's marriage to Phil Hand, who died
in combat with a kamikaze pilot. World War I makes the world of "The
Window" anachronistic; Thomas Daniel Young points out that the community in which Laurel grew up and in which her parents had their place
is rapidly disappearing, replaced by a suburban lifestyle of divorce and
dispersal. Ruth Vande Kieft begins her discussion of *The Optimist's Daughter* with an analysis of Welty's use of time, arguing that "both narrator
and characters are fixed on time: scarcely a page is without direct or
oblique reference to it." Welty's comment on Woolf's "Time Passes"
section—"time gets in"—describes *The Optimist's Daughter* equally well.[4]

The most important connection between *Delta Wedding* and *The Optimist's Daughter*, a connection that sheds much light on the novel's relationship to *To the Lighthouse*, is the similarity between Laura McRaven
and Laurel McKelva Hand. The echo in their very names points to the

3. DuPlessis, *Writing Beyond Ending*, 60.

4. Thomas Daniel Young, "Social Form and Social Order: An Examination of *The
Optimist's Daughter*," in *Critical Essays*, ed. Prenshaw, 381; Vande Kieft, *Eudora Welty*
(rev. ed), 165–66; Welty, Foreword to *To the Lighthouse*, x.

more substantial parallels in their situations and characters. Each protagonist has lost her mother and seeks to come to terms with this loss in the course of the novel. Of course, Laurel Hand's loss is compounded by the deaths of her husband and father, bringing issues of loss and death to the center of *The Optimist's Daughter,* while Laura McRaven's loss remains marginalized, diminished by the pastoral world of Shellmound. Both Laura and Laurel begin their respective novels as outsiders, which casts them into observer roles vis à vis their communities. Although Laurel returns to her childhood home, she returns as an outsider, as one who has chosen to live and work elsewhere. With the death of her parents, Laurel loses her standing in the Mount Salus community, as Mrs. Pease makes clear: "Once you leave after this, you'll always come back as a visitor. . . . Feel free, of course—but it was always my opinion that people don't really want visitors" (*OD,* 133). Laurel's and Laura's similar personalities also fit them for the observer role: quiet, introspective, shy. As Michael Kreyling points out, these characteristics are shared as well by Woolf's Lily Briscoe: "[Laurel] is like Lily Briscoe in many ways—introspective, sensitive to the bustling and fighting around her, yet reluctant to leap out of herself and into the ring. She is like Lily also in a way that is significant for the novel; Laurel's discovery of the unifying stroke that coaxes contradictions into harmony, the gift of an inspired moment of her heart's attention, fulfills and climaxes the book." [5]

Like the observers in so many Welty novels, Laura McRaven and Laurel McKelva Hand are artist figures, a role that again connects them closely with Woolf's Lily Briscoe. Leslie Hankins suggests that the sort of quiet but passionate personality of these characters and their position as outsiders are important features of the Weltian artist: "Welty's female artist figures come to life on the thresholds as witnesses, investigators, rapt seekers, examining domestic models as well as artistic." [6] But Laura McRaven is a child of nine, and her role as an artist is thus limited. Laurel, "a professional designer of fabrics in Chicago" (*OD,* 25), is the culmination of Welty's female artist figures. *The Optimist's Daughter* brings to-

---

5. Kreyling, *Eudora Welty's Achievement of Order,* 166.

6. Leslie Kathleen Hankins, "Alas, Alack! Or a Lass, a Lack? Quarrels of Gender in the Revisionist *Kunstlerroman*: Eudora Welty's *The Golden Apples,*" *Mississippi Quarterly,* XLIV (1991), 397.

gether *To the Lighthouse*'s concerns with the family and the female artist
into the psyche and experience of a single character. Unlike Lily Briscoe,
who merely observes the Ramsays' family dynamics, Laurel is both child
and artist, and her struggles with memory and art fuse the two parts of
Woolf's "The Lighthouse," divided as it is between Lily and James. Like
James Ramsay, Laurel must find some way of uniting in herself the polar
opposition of her parents' characters; like Lily Briscoe, Laurel must overcome the obstacles facing the woman artist and learn to create the patterns that will give meaning to her life.

THE NOVEL AS ELEGY

As she began planning *To the Lighthouse,* Woolf wrote in her diary, "I
have an idea that I will invent a new name for my books to supplant
'novel.' A new ——— by Virginia Woolf. But what? Elegy?" (*WD*, 78).
Both *To the Lighthouse* and *The Optimist's Daughter* are elegiac narratives
that consciously explore strategies the living use to survive and understand death, loss, and impermanence. More particularly, these two novels
function as elegies because they are autobiographical. Virginia Woolf in
To the Lighthouse and Eudora Welty in *The Optimist's Daughter* re-create
their own parents through language in order to come to terms with their
parents' deaths. In the early stages of composing her novel, Woolf commented on its autobiographical origins: "This is going to be fairly short;
to have father's character done complete in it; and mother's; and St. Ives;
and childhood; and all the usual things I try to put in—life, death, etc.
But the centre is father's character, sitting in a boat, reciting We perished,
each alone, while he crushes a dying mackerel" (*WD*, 75). Once Woolf
completed the work, her mother had replaced her father as the narrative's
center, but the autobiographical and elegiac impulse and purpose re-
mained.

Speaking of *The Optimist's Daughter,* Welty comments, "It's the first
thing I've ever done that has direct autobiographical information in it.
I'm not sure that was right—the mother is based on my mother. The
boys are her brothers . . . and the West Virginia part is set in her own
country" (*C,* 69). As readers of *One Writer's Beginnings* discover, much

more than the mother and her family is autobiographical in this novel. The daughter's departure and her guilt over leaving the family home, the personalities of the mother and father, and many other qualities and details in *The Optimist's Daughter* grow out of Welty's own experience as a daughter and an artist.[7]

Of course, it would be a disservice to call either *To the Lighthouse* or *The Optimist's Daughter* strict autobiography. In her foreword, Welty describes the relationship between fiction and autobiography in *To the Lighthouse:*

> The setting of *To the Lighthouse* is generally supposed to be much like the place at St. Ives in Cornwall where the Stephen family spent the summers during Virginia Woolf's childhood; and the portraits of Mr. and Mrs. Ramsay are said to derive from Leslie and Julia Stephen, the author's parents. However great a part recollection played in informing the novel, what connects *To the Lighthouse* to autobiography seems meteorological in nature. Not slow recollection so much as a bolt of lightning runs between them; we enter a world that is lit by its flash and play and under its heavenly signs is transformed.[8]

As Welty well knows, the relationship between fiction and autobiography is complex, and the transformation of life into art is not a matter of simple representation but has to do with the construction of patterns of meaning and value, identity and relation, as much as with plot and character.

For each author, the act of writing these novels had autobiographical implications as well as origins. Woolf explains, "I used to think of him and mother daily; but writing the *Lighthouse* laid them in my mind. And now [father] comes back sometimes, but differently. (I believe this to be true—that I was obsessed by them both, unhealthily; and writing of them was a necessary act)" (*WD,* 135). Welty wrote her novel about a daughter's coming to terms with her parents' death in the year following

---

7. See Floyd C. Watkins, "The Journey to Baltimore in *The Optimist's Daughter,*" *Mississippi Quarterly,* XXXVIII (1985), 435–40. Watkins traces in detail the autobiographical sources of Becky McKelva's trip down the river with her dying father.

8. Welty, Foreword to *To the Lighthouse,* vii.

her mother's death. For Welty the act of writing about her parents was an act of recovery and discovery rather than one of exorcism, a point she makes clearly in *One Writer's Beginnings:* "It seems to me, writing of my parents now in my seventies, that I see continuities in their lives that weren't visible to me when they were living. Even at the times that have left me my most vivid memories of them, there were connections between them that escaped me. Could it be . . . I can better see their lives— or any lives I know—today because I'm a fiction writer? See them not as fiction, certainly—see them, perhaps, as even greater mysteries than I knew" (*OWB*, 90).

Although Welty finds continuity in writing of her parents where Woolf finds freedom from her parents' hold on her, in each case the point of writing about one's parents and about the past is not simply to preserve it. The focus of the writing is its effect on the writer. As DiBattista says, "*To the Lighthouse* is an elegiac narrative that treats its subject—the dead mother and father—exclusively in terms of the surviving daughter, the implied, anonymous narrator of the novel. . . . Woolf's elegy thus occasions a double celebration: the dead are transfigured (they come back, but differently) and the living descendant discovers an independent voice and a genuine artistic vocation." [9] In *The Optimist's Daughter*, the "implied, anonymous narrator" becomes the surviving daughter as Welty attaches narrative point of view to Laurel's perspective and sensibility. The creation of voice and vision (though not, in Welty's fiction, independent, but connected) is situated in the character of the woman artist.

But neither *To the Lighthouse* nor *The Optimist's Daughter* is pure elegy in the sense that Milton's "Lycidas" or Shelley's "Adonais" are; these are ultimately comic novels. Not only do they stress continuity and look toward the future, but they include humor and laughter. By bringing the elegiac into contact with comedy and laughter, both Woolf and Welty *carnivalize* it, to use Bakhtin's term. An elegy in the traditional sense serves, as Bakhtin explains, to fix and distance its objects: "They withdraw themselves . . . from the present day with all its inconclusiveness, its indecision, its openness, its potential for re-thinking and re-evaluating. They are raised to the valorized plane of the past and assume there a

9. DiBattista, *The Fables of Anon*, 68.

finished quality." But within the context of the novel, the elegy is "dialogized, permeated with laughter, irony, humor, elements of self-parody
and finally—this is the most important thing—the novel inserts into
[the elegy] an indeterminacy, a certain semantic openendedness, a living
contact with unfinished, still-evolving contemporary reality." These
comic, parodic, irreverent qualities of the novel Bakhtin terms *carnival*
because of their roots in the culture of folk humor of the Middle Ages
and Renaissance. Characterized by laughter, carnival is essentially comic,
associated with transgression, travesty, and "the destruction of the established hierarchy." In *Rabelais and His World* Bakhtin describes the power
of carnival laughter: "Laughter liberates not only from external censor-
ship but first of all from the great interior censor; it liberates from the
fear that developed in man during thousands of years: fear of the sacred,
of prohibitions, of the past, of power. It unveils the material bodily principle in its true meaning. Laughter opened men's eyes on that which is
new, on the future. . . . Laughter showed the world anew in its gayest
and most sober aspects." [10]

In *Comedy and the Woman Writer*, Judy Little uses Bakhtinian language
to theorize a form of feminist comedy that is similar to Bakhtin's carnival.
She argues that the kind of comic imagery that Woolf uses "is usually
that of festive license or of an important 'passage' in life. Further, such
imagery—imagery of revolt and inversion—is ordinarily not resolved in
the fiction of these authors. In this respect the imagery differs from the
license of traditional festive holiday, and certainly it differs from rounded-
off comic fiction in which the hero is ultimately reintegrated into society.
The comedy I am considering here is renegade comedy. It mocks the
deepest possible norms, norms four thousand years old." Specifically discussing the element of comedy in *To the Lighthouse*, Little points to the
iconoclastic quality of Woolf's novel: "[The] novel could well be called
a comedy of myth, for the mocking voice frequently satirizes the archetypal fantasies of characters, or looks at a ritual occasion through mythic
metaphors. In either case, the metaphors and the fantasies draw upon
mythic imagery (not merely the external manner of an era), and this

10. Bakhtin, *The Dialogic Imagination*, 18, 7; Mikhail Bakhtin, *Rabelais and His World*,
trans. Helen Iswolsky (Bloomington, Ind., 1984), 237, 94.

imagery is mocked. The effect is that of toppling an archetypal icon, something venerated for centuries." As Dale M. Bauer explains, "To open another's discourse [the discourse of myth or of any authoritative system] is to make it vulnerable to change, to exposure, to carnival." [11]

It is this feminist, carnivalized form of the elegy that Woolf and Welty exploit in their novels. In *To the Lighthouse* the parents are not distanced and memorialized; rather, they are mocked as much as they are honored. Woolf reveals their absurdities along with their dignity. Thus Mr. Ramsay's bursts of Romantic poetry and his vision of himself as "the leader of the doomed expedition" (*TL,* 57) appear ludicrous in their melodrama and undercut his mythic stature as the father. Carnival reveals itself as well in Mrs. Ramsay's contemplation of Paul and Minta's engagement at the dinner table: "This will celebrate the occasion—a curious sense rising in her, at once freakish and tender, of celebrating a festival, as if two emotions were called up in her, one profound—for what could be more serious than the love of man for woman, what more commanding, more impressive, bearing in its bosom the seeds of death; at the same time these lovers, these people entering into illusion glittering eyed, must be danced round with mockery, decorated with garlands" (*TL,* 151). The dinner, though Mrs. Ramsay sees it as a celebration of permanence, of that which "is immune from change" (*TL,* 158), is itself a celebration on the eve of great change, the change brought on by the First World War, which marks the transition from the pastoral fantasy of "The Window" to the dehumanized chaos of "Time Passes."

"Time Passes," with its stress on flux, change, and "indeterminacy," is almost pure carnival. Human tragedy is reduced to parenthetical statement, whereas human comedy in the character of Mrs. McNab cooperates with the forces of chaos and darkness. Carnival, explains Bakhtin, is "intimately related to life–death–birth." [12] As Lily discovers, thinking of the dead Mrs. Ramsay in "The Lighthouse," within the carnivalized world of the novel, the dead do not stay dead, do not maintain their distance and fixity: "It had seemed so safe, thinking of [Mrs. Ramsay].

11. Judy Little, *Comedy and the Woman Writer: Woolf, Spark, and Feminism* (Lincoln, Nebr., 1983), 1, 58; Bauer, *Feminist Dialogics,* 673.

12. Bakhtin, *Rabelais and His World,* 149.

Ghost, air, nothingness, a thing you could play with easily and safely at any time of day or night, she had been that, and then suddenly she put her hand out and wrung the heart thus" (*TL*, 266). Carnival transgresses boundaries between the living and the dead, between the stylized dignity of myth and the absurdities of everyday life, between comedy and tragedy. *To the Lighthouse* mocks while celebrating the dead, and thus calls into question the power of the parents, the power of death, the power of myth, and diminishes the distance of elegy.

The Optimist's Daughter takes this carnivalization even further as Welty makes it a central subject of her novel. The Mardi Gras setting of Part 1 is a literal carnival, one that marks (and mocks) the boundary between the sacred and profane worlds. Bakhtin associates the start of "legalized" carnival with the celebrations surrounding Lent: "As we have seen, free laughter was related to feasts and was to a certain extent limited by the time allotted to feast days. It coincided with the permission for meat, fat, and sexual intercourse. This festive liberation of laughter and body was in sharp contrast with the stringencies of Lent which had preceded or were to follow."[13] The New Orleans Mardi Gras celebration is an example of Bakhtinian carnival in action. As Laurel's father's death transfigures her life, the Mardi Gras carnival, with its multiple processions, transfigures the city and prefigures the comic funeral scenes of Part 2.[14] The festival undercuts and mocks Laurel's tragedy, and she hears in it "the unmistakable sound of hundreds, of thousands, of people *blundering*" (*OD*, 55). By contrast, Fay, the novel's most purely comic character, finds her milieu in it: "Fay grabbed Laurel's arm as she would have grabbed any stranger's. 'I saw a man—I saw a man and he was dressed up like a skeleton and his date was in a long white dress, with snakes for hair,

---

13. *Ibid.*, 89.

14. In *One Writer's Beginnings* Welty discusses the importance of processions, characteristic of Bakhtin's carnival, to her fiction: "It is not for nothing that an ominous feeling often attaches itself to a procession. . . . In films and stories we see spectacles forming in the street and parades coming from around the corner, and we know to greet them with distrust and apprehension: their intent is still to be revealed. . . . I never resisted it when, in almost every story I ever wrote, some parade or procession, impromptu or ceremonious, comic or mocking or funereal, has risen up to mark some stage of the story's unfolding. They've started from far back" (*OWB*, 37).

holding up a bunch of lilies! Coming down the steps of that house like they're just starting out!' Then she cried out again, the longing, or the anger, of her whole life all in her voice at one time, 'Is it the Carnival?' " (*OD*, 55). Robert Brinkmeyer, Jr., notes Fay's affinity with the carnival spirit of Mardi Gras, pointing out that "her very name (Wanda—'wand'—a magical staff; and Fay—'fairy') suggests her closeness to carnival revelry" and that her "birthday falls on Mardi Gras day." [15]

In a similar way, the presence of the Dalzells in the hospital waiting room undercuts Laurel's sense of the seriousness of her father's illness. In their celebration of the present, of unconscious life, they are members of "the great, interrelated family of those who never know the meaning of what has happened to them" (*OD*, 103). Fay is right at home with the Dalzells, but Laurel is horrified in the face of their cheerful oblivion, their carnival: "It seemed to Laurel that in another moment the whole waiting room would dissolve itself in waiting-room laughter" (*OD*, 51). Neither Fay nor the Dalzells, nor Welty's narrative, take death as seriously as Laurel believes they should.

The funeral in Part 2 becomes a carnival as well, as the Presbyterians of Mount Salus engage in a contest with the Baptist Chisoms. Laurel wants the event to be one of respect and propriety, and she would like to limit severely the ways in which mourners could speak of her father. She seeks the sort of elegy Bakhtin speaks of when he says, "The dead are loved in a different way. They are removed from the sphere of contact, one can and indeed must speak of them in a different style. Language about the dead is stylistically quite distinct from language about the living." [16] The Mount Salus mourners, whose words Laurel criticizes, speak of the Judge as one of the dead, even though their eulogizing does not meet Laurel's standards. At the funeral they have already begun to build up apocrypha and legend, placing Judge McKelva in a removed and "valorized past." This process is disrupted, however, by the Chisoms' arrival and by Fay McKelva's mourning. Throwing herself into the casket, Fay violates the dead's removal "from the sphere of contact," and she

15. Robert H. Brinkmeyer, Jr., "New Orleans, Mardi Gras, and Eudora Welty's *The Optimist's Daughter*," *Mississippi Quarterly*, XLIV (1991), 435.

16. Bakhtin, *The Dialogic Imagination*, 20.

speaks to the Judge as if he were still alive: "Oh hon," she cries, "get up, get out of there"; and she asks him, "Can't you hear me, hon?" (*OD*, 103). Fay's behavior is a comic parody of mourning that undercuts and mocks Laurel's grief and her insistence that others "*remember* right" (*OD*, 102).

At the cemetery Laurel's vision of her parents resting together beneath the big camellia is destroyed by Fay's plans: "How could the biggest fool think I was going to bury my husband with his old wife? He's going in the new part" (*OD*, 108). Humor and temporality replace the comfortable and dignified permanence Laurel sees in the cemetery's old section, where "winged angels and life-sized effigies of bygone citizens in old-fashioned dress" stand among the trees "like a familiar set of passengers collected on deck of a ship, on which they all knew each other—bonafide members of a small local excursion, embarked on a voyage that is always returning in dreams" (*OD*, 108). By comic contrast in the new part of the cemetery, "indestructible plastic Christmas poinsettias" (*OD*, 109) mark the few new graves, and the noise of the highway (an image of transience) drowns out the burial ceremony.

In the early sections of the novel Laurel seeks the distance of elegy, what Bakhtin describes as "a valorized past of beginnings and peak times. This past is distanced, finished and closed like a circle. . . . [It] is not relative to the present or to the future." [17] She seeks fixity and permanence, especially in her memory of her parents and their relationship. But the novel consistently uses comedy to undercut and mock her attempts to fix the past and memory. Fay, the major threat to Laurel's fixed memory of her parents' relationship, is an almost purely carnival figure. The most physical, "bodily" character in the text, she is represented again and again through references to her body: she points to her breastbone, drums her fists upon her temples, and tries to "lay hands" on the dying Judge. Her brightly colored clothing draws attention to her physicality. Carnival is characterized by an emphasis on the body and bodily functions, undercutting the elegy's disembodied images, and the language of Welty's novel is filled with references to the body, most often associated

17. *Ibid.*, 19.

with Fay.[18] She possesses a sensuality and sexuality absent from the rest of the characters, a sexuality, moreover, that Laurel finds threatening and seeks to ignore.

Fay's pink-satin bed serves as a garish reminder of her sexual nature, a transgression of the traditional restraint in the McKelva home. Her mere presence disrupts Mount Salus' social order.[19] As the women of the town complain to Laurel, Fay neither plays bridge nor cooks. "You got a peep at her origins," says Mrs. Pease (*OD*, 126), for whom origins are absolute designators of worth. But origins do not count to Fay. She rejects the past, lying to Laurel that her family is dead and later proclaiming, "The past isn't a thing to me" (*OD*, 207). As Bakhtin notes, the comic has little to do with the past: "Here the role of memory is minimal; in the comic world there is nothing for memory and tradition to do."[20] Fay's presence destroys Laurel's control of the past, forcing her to reevaluate and recreate her own origins, just as Fay's family thwarts her attempts to control the funeral.

Fay is thus the catalyst that initiates Laurel's movement out of her state of living death toward a reawakened life. I do not mean to suggest that *The Optimist's Daughter* endorses Fay's approach to life. In fact, in an interview with Jan Nordby Gretlund, Welty says that "there was 'evil' in Fay" (*C*, 227). But several critics have commented on the vitality she brings to the novel; it is the vitality of carnival.[21] Without it, the novel would lack the energy and momentum that propel Laurel forward into her discovery/creation of the meaning of her experience. Despite this energy, Welty's novel suggests that the carnival perspective represented most fully in the character of Fay is not sufficient, not complete. Fay is

18. Bev Byrne, "A Return to the Source: Eudora Welty's *The Robber Bride-groom* and *The Optimist's Daughter*," in *Critical Essays on Eudora Welty*, ed. Turner and Harding, 249.

19. Fuller, "Making a Scene," 310–18, describes Fay's sexuality as a performance designed to challenge social hierarchy and argues that it "reveals the interconnection of power, identity and sexuality within the arena of marriage" (313).

20. Bakhtin, *The Dialogic Imagination*, 23.

21. See John Edward Hardy, "Marrying Down in Eudora Welty's Novels," in *Critical Essays*, ed. Prenshaw, 118; Ruth Weston, "The Feminine and Feminist Texts of Eudora Welty's *The Optimist's Daughter*," *South Central Review*, IV (1987), 83–84.

also superficial, petty, and lacking in understanding and compassion, two of the most significant virtues in the world of Welty's fiction. Faced with the fact of her father's second marriage and Fay's presence in and even ownership of the family home, Laurel must come to terms with the drawbacks, the lacks inherent in her own approach to the world and to the people around her. She must negotiate some sort of middle ground between her own attachment to a fixed and distanced past and Fay's total rejection of the past, between her own disembodied, detached stance and Fay's completely embodied and self-centered position in relation to others. The episode describing Laurel's fear of the pigeons suggests that Laurel has feared both physical and emotional intimacy since childhood. As a child, visiting her mother's family "up home," Laurel had watched, overcome by horror, a pair of pigeons "sticking their beaks down each other's throats, gagging each other, eating out of each other's craws, swallowing down all over again what had been swallowed before: they were taking turns" (*OD*, 166). The child Laurel's comment on this behavior, "They convinced her that they could not escape each other and could not themselves be escaped from" (*OD*, 166), is echoed in the adult Laurel's comment about her own behavior during her father's death: "I did not any longer believe that anyone could be saved, anyone at all. Not from others" (*OD*, 170). The emotional and physical distance she maintains from her dying father, in contrast to Fay's giving him cigarettes and finally shaking him, results from a circumspect and suspicious view of human intimacy.

In the course of the novel, Laurel journeys from this isolation to a fuller understanding and acceptance of human connections. On the night before the funeral, Laurel's memory of her parents and their relationship consists entirely of disembodied voices:

> When Laurel was a child, in this room and in this bed where she lay now, she closed her eyes like this and the rhythmic, nighttime sound of the two beloved reading voices came rising in turn up the stairs every night to reach her. She could hardly fall asleep, and she tried to keep awake, for pleasure. She cared for her own books, but she cared more for theirs, which meant their voices. In the lateness of the night, their two voices reading to each other where she could hear them, never letting a silence divide or interrupt

them, combined into one unceasing voice and wrapped her around as she listened, as still as if she were asleep. She was sent to sleep under a velvety cloak of words, richly patterned and stitched with gold, straight out of a fairy tale, while they went reading on into her dreams. (*OD*, 70–71)

Rather than holding a mature view of her parents' relationship, Laurel indulges in a child's view that stresses protection and comfort, ignoring sexuality, conflict, pain, and ambiguity. The numerous references to sleep in this section underscore the muted, flat quality of the narrative in the early portion of the novel: in the early sections of *The Optimist's Daughter*, Laurel herself is a sleepwalker, a somnambulist, to use one of Welty's favorite words, who resists awakening into maturity.

During her night alone in the house with her memories, Laurel travels toward a mature understanding and acceptance of human intimacy. She comes to see the complexity, the mixture of love and betrayal, in her parents' relationship, in her relationship with her parents, and in her brief relationship with her husband. As she progresses towards her new understanding, the disembodied voices are replaced by memories having to do with hands. Laurel remembers sitting with her parents during her mother's illness, remembers "her mother holding and holding onto their hands, her own and her father's holding onto her mother's, long after there was nothing more to be said" (*OD*, 177). She recalls, as well, "her mother holding her hands before her eyes, very close, so that she seemed to be seeing them, the empty, working fingers. 'Poor hands in winter, when she came back from the well—bleeding from the ice, from the ice!' her mother cried. 'Who, Mother?' Laurel asked. '*My* mother!' she cried accusingly" (*OD*, 177).

Laurel's desire for her mother to protect her from the consequences of her father's second marriage is replaced by compassion for her mother, an emotion that ushers Laurel back into a living perception of relationships and sense of her own connection to the other people in her life. Her revelation is carried forward in Part 4 as she remembers her husband, Phil Hand. Phil, who "had large, good hands" (*OD*, 188) in keeping with his name, had taught Laurel that love is more than refuge and safety. "Protection, like self-protection, fell away from her like all one garment, some anachronism foolishly saved from childhood" (*OD*, 187–88).

Here again, the formal, distanced remove of elegy is carnivalized, brought into contact with the present and the body and made vulnerable and alive. Laurel's marriage, the past that she had "sealed away into its perfection," Laurel raises up "by her own hands" (*OD*, 181), and "*he looked at her, Phil himself—here waiting, all the time, Lazarus. He looked at her out of eyes wild with the craving for his unlived life, with mouth open like a funnel's*" (*OD*, 181). Lazarus, returning bodily from the grave, transgressing the ultimate boundary between life and death, is a carnival image. By bringing the past into contact with the present, by embodying human intimacy, Laurel makes of memory a living thing, "vulnerable to the living moment" (*OD*, 207). She discovers that "the fantasies of dying could be no stranger than the fantasies of living. Surviving is perhaps the strangest fantasy of them all" (*OD*, 189). Carnival, in Bakhtin's words, "does not deny seriousness but purifies and completes it. Laughter purifies from dogmatism, from the intolerant and the petrified; it liberates from fanaticism and pedantry, from fear and intimidation, from didacticism, naivete and illusion, from the single meaning, the single level, from sentimentality. Laughter does not permit seriousness to atrophy and to be torn away from the one being, forever incomplete. It restores this ambivalent wholeness."[22] Laurel's encounter with carnival restores her to a wholeness that is vital in its connection to others yet ambivalent in its vulnerability to pain.

NEGOTIATING DUALITIES

To convey the growth of Laurel's understanding, Welty pushes to an extreme the "subjective" mode she praises in her foreword to *To the Lighthouse* and uses in *Delta Wedding*. "The real action," says Welty of *The Optimist's Daughter*, "is . . . all interior" (*C*, 284).[23] In this novel, the

22. Bakhtin, *Rabelais and His World*, 122–23.

23. That Welty, like Woolf, is an innovative novelist whose concern with the form of the novel is evidenced in her work, is obvious in the most cursory comparison of the narrative strategies she uses in *Losing Battles* and *The Optimist's Daughter*. Whereas her goal in the first of these is to represent everything externally, in *The Optimist's Daughter*, she works in an opposing mode, representing everything through an interior narrative.

subjective is reduced to a single character's point of view. Rather than break up the narrative perspective among a number of characters as she does in *Delta Wedding,* Welty presents the entire work to us through a narrative perception closely allied with Laurel McKelva Hand. Although the novel opens with what sounds at first like a detached, third-person narrator, by the second page Judge McKelva is referred to as "Laurel's father" (*OD,* 10), and the narrative begins to focus on details significant to Laurel. As Welty explains in an interview with Charlotte Capers, "It's really an interior story of what went on in a young widow's mind in response to grief and loss and her adjustment to facing up to it, and acceptance of the meaning of love in her life and affection" (*C,* 115).

Even more than in Woolf's *To the Lighthouse,* the imagery and tone of *The Optimist's Daughter* directly reflect the protagonist's mental and emotional state. As in Woolf's *The Waves,* in *The Optimist's Daughter* the external world becomes an extension of the protagonist's internal reality. Thus the seeming flatness and simplicity of the first section, which consists primarily of observation rather than contemplation, results from Laurel's emotionally frozen condition. Like Lily Briscoe on her return to the house in the Hebrides after Mrs. Ramsay's death, Laurel cannot feel. But while Lily struggles to feel, or at least to come to terms with not feeling, Laurel fights feeling, holds it at bay; she is engaged in a personal "cold war" against emotion. To gain access to Laurel's reaction to her father's operation and death, we must depend on what Laurel notices and doesn't notice, on the presence and absence of narrative images, rather than on the thoughts and feelings that she does not express. The very absence of such mental commentary is more important to an understanding of Laurel's character and condition than are the few instances of reflection we do get. While Fay cries, yells, spits, and demands attention and sympathy, Laurel listens and watches. She notices the physical changes in her father, the design in the tiling on the hospital floor, the play of light on the river; she listens to the conversations of the Dalzells in the waiting room and the chirping of frogs outside her hotel room. But she studiously does not react to her father's illness and death.

The most commentary we get from Laurel about her view of the events of Part 1 comes from two rather oblique statements. First, Laurel tells Dr. Courtland that "some things don't bear going into" (*OD,* 53),

a remark that gives the reader insight into Laurel's remote, detached stance and the flat, minimalist tone of the narrative. Later, as she and Fay drive through Mardi Gras revelry on their way to their hotel, Laurel mentally comments on the festival: "She heard the crowd noise, the unmistakable sound of hundreds, of thousands of people *blundering*" (*OD*, 55), a comment that conveys Laurel's strong need for control and emotional reserve.

The clearest indication Welty gives us of Laurel's emotional reaction to her father's death comes from the imagery of the penultimate paragraph of Part 1: "As the train left the black swamp and pulled out into the space of Pontchartrain, the window filled with a featureless sky over pale smooth water, where a seagull was hanging with wings fixed, like a stopped clock on a wall" (*OD*, 57). The static, bland, muted images indicate that Laurel is not feeling; she is frozen, fixed in time. Laurel, like Laura McRaven and Lily Briscoe before her, must reclaim her grief and experience her loss before she can return to life. What Carolyn Williams says of Lily Briscoe's return to feeling in *To the Lighthouse* is true as well of Laurel's condition in *The Optimist's Daughter*: "Emptiness and numbness seem the necessary precondition of emotion, of 'feeling' that is pointedly corporeal. A palpable absence seems necessary to conjure the illusion of presence, as if a space must be cleared inside in order to become the medium of exchange between the living and the dead. 'Feeling' seems to be a dynamic of emptying and enclosing."[24]

Laurel's passage from empty numbness to feeling is the focus of each section of *The Optimist's Daughter*. The structure of the novel, described by Young as "three almost equal parts and a brief conclusion," reflects the three-part structure of *To the Lighthouse*. In both novels the first section establishes the social and familial order that designates insiders and outsiders and demarcates expected gender roles. Although the comic, social tone of the funeral section of *The Optimist's Daughter* differs significantly from the "Time Passes" section of *To the Lighthouse,* a passage stripped of most human perception, the two sections have much the same function in their respective novels. Just as absence, death, and chaos lie at the center of *To the Lighthouse,* they lie as well at the center of *The*

---

24. Williams, "Virginia Woolf's Rhetoric of Enclosure," 44.

Optimist's Daughter. In spite of the comic elements of the funeral, for Laurel McKelva Hand the experience is one of violation, chaos, destruction, and loss, comparable to that of Woolf's "Time Passes." Challenging the social and familial structures, the funeral calls into question Laurel's view of the past and therefore her sense of self. Emptiness lies at the center of each novel, but as Williams says of *To the Lighthouse,* "loss, grief, and mourning intersect with strategies of self definition."[25] The third section of each novel examines this intersection.

Because *The Optimist's Daughter* follows the changes in Laurel's psyche and emotions that result from the novel's events, each section takes on a slightly different tone as Laurel progresses from numbness to life. In Part 2 Laurel is stripped even of her control of the narrative by the community that takes over the funeral, a public, communal event. What we do see in the funeral scenes of Part 2, as Laurel begins the slow return to feeling, is the clash between her private world of grief and the social world of Mount Salus and the funeral. In the second section of *The Optimist's Daughter* Welty again makes use of the chorus that is so important to *Losing Battles* and Virginia Woolf's *The Waves.* As Welty explains, *The Optimist's Daughter* progresses by means of "a series of confrontations, of only four or five people, plus a chorus of small townspeople who come to a funeral and come from here, there, and everywhere to speak as a chorus about love and death and so on" (*C,* 115).

Although the events surrounding the funeral are still presented through Laurel's point of view, Welty uses Miss Adele's remarks to provide an external commentary on the public ritual of death. When Laurel complains that the mourners are "misrepresenting" and "falsifying" (*OD,* 101) her father with their stories of heroic exploits, Miss Adele defends them, explaining, "They're trying to say for a man that his life is over" (*OD,* 100). Laurel is angered by the rivalry over her father and over the appropriate display of grief that develops between the Mount Salus mourners and the Chisoms, but she remains blind to the rivalry she engages in. When she claims, "I'm his daughter. I want what people say now to be the truth" (*OD,* 101), she wants her perception of Judge

25. Young, "Social Form and Social Order," in *Critical Essays,* ed. Prenshaw, 369; Williams, "Virginia Woolf's Rhetoric of Enclosure," 46.

McKelva as her father to prevail over the community's reading of him as a public figure and over Fay's interpretation of him as her husband. This section of Welty's novel dramatizes competing interpretations and readings of the Judge's life to suggest that Laurel's "truth" about her father is just as limited, just as subjective, as the community's. Like the Mount Salus mourners, Laurel seeks a view of the past and of her father's personality that will confirm her identity and maintain her personal sense of continuity. Laurel is, in this section, interested in memory only insofar as it can protect her from time and change. Her desire to protect her father from the mourners is really a longing to preserve inviolate her sense of identity built upon her memory of her parents, a memory that has been threatened by the events at the funeral.

In the third section of both *The Optimist's Daughter* and *To the Lighthouse*, Laurel McKelva Hand and Lily Briscoe return to feeling through experiencing a profound loss. Through struggling with the dead, they return to life. The dialogue between the living and the dead, between the present and the past, is central to both novels. In contrast to Part 1 of *The Optimist's Daughter*, Part 3 is compounded mostly of reflection rather than observation. As the section progresses and Laurel's emotional thaw begins, observation initiates memory. But at the start of the section, Laurel still fights to defend and preserve her version of the truth, her view of the past and of her parents. Parts 3 and 4 chronicle the freeing of memory through grief and the return to life through coming to terms with death. In Barbara Harrell Carson's words, "*The Optimist's Daughter* demonstrates that there are more ways than one to be dead in this world and more ways than one to be alive." Welty's novel moves, as DiBattista says of *To the Lighthouse*, "from a dream of childhood through a nightmare of bereavement into the dream of freedom."[26]

Each novel establishes an intimate connection between the house and the deceased loved ones. Lily sees Mrs. Ramsay's death and absence echoed in the empty steps, while Laurel seeks her father in the library and recalls her dead mother in the sewing room. As William McMillen points out, "We must recognize the struggles of the living to come to grips

---

26. Carson, *Two Pictures at Once in Her Frame*, 139; DiBattista, *The Fables of Anon*, 110.

with not only the human past but also the home as an on-going symbol of the past. Homes become the holders of memories, store houses which have an almost magical power to attract the families."[27] This power explains Laurel's insistence upon avoiding those rooms that Fay has redecorated and removing from the house what signs of Fay she can. Laurel sees Fay's presence in the house as a desecration of memory, of her parents' relationship, and of Laurel's childhood.

Laurel's attempts to come to terms with her past, to find answers to the questions raised by her father's marriage, death, and funeral, therefore focus on the house in which she grew up. McMillen explains, "Laurel thus is left alone for one final stay in her family home. Her desire to find the past, to escape Fay's superficial changes, leads her upstairs as if she is circling-in on the very heart of her home, her family and her past."[28] At the center of this circling-in she arrives at the sewing room, where she discovers through memory her dead mother and her own childhood. The circling imagery and the dynamic of emptiness and fullness, absence and presence, echo the imagery of Lily Briscoe's experience in "The Lighthouse": "Suddenly, the empty drawing-room steps, the frill of the chair inside, the puppy tumbling on the terrace, the whole wave and whisper of the garden became like curves and arabesques flourishing round a centre of complete emptiness" (TL, 266). In each case the emptiness is filled as memory returns presence and life: Mrs. Ramsay and Laurel's mother, Becky McKelva, take on a life within their respective texts as full as that of the "living" characters. After the anguish of wanting and not having, Lily calls out Mrs. Ramsay's name and then sees her: "Mrs. Ramsay—it was part of her perfect goodness—sat there quite simply, in the chair, flicked her needles to and fro, knitted her reddish-brown stocking, cast her shadow on the step. There she sat" (TL, 300).

In the new absence created by Judge McKelva's death, Becky McKelva comes to life in The Optimist's Daughter, from her experiences as a young girl taking her dying father to Baltimore to her quoting of poetry from the McGuffey's Fifth Reader during her final illness. Welty notes in a

27. William McMillen, "Circling-In: The Concept of Home in Eudora Welty's *Losing Battles* and *The Optimist's Daughter*," in *A Still Moment: Essays on the Art of Eudora Welty*, ed. John F. Desmond (Metuchen, N.J., 1978), 113.

28. *Ibid.*, 114.

1978 interview with Martha van Noppen that Becky is more important to the novel than is the Judge, though it is his death that initiates Laurel's sojourn into the past (*C,* 242). The recovery of her mother leads Laurel to the more important and more startling recovery of her dead husband, Phil. Ruth Weston suggests that the novel "expands with many narratives called forth by the presence of the absent voice of Judge Clinton Mc-Kelva. The novel resembles Faulkner's *As I Lay Dying* as an extended metaphor for the presence of absence, the presence of the corpse and the absence of life, but also the presence of the words that are spoken to represent that absence and other absences." The loss and death at the center of each novel provide the necessary condition for recovery and creativity in each. As Carolyn Williams says, "But what arises as an invocation of loss, emptiness, and vacancy takes shape and form around that center. Emptiness generates form in these Woolfian [and Weltian] elegies, and form depends on emptiness at the center." Lily's and Laurel's experiences depend on this paradox, as do the structures of these two novels. Welty sees this movement between these opposites as creating the narrative rhythm of *To the Lighthouse*: "There is a felt rhythm, too, underlying the novel's structure and forming a pattern of waking and sleeping, presence and absence, living and living no longer, between clamorous memory and lapses of mind, between the rushing in of love and the loosening of the hand in sleep."[29]

This same rhythm is at work in Welty's own novel. The complex dynamic of presence and absence, fullness and emptiness, and form and chaos frees Laurel from her need to cling to her limited, static reading of the past and allows her to move toward a creative self-definition. Paradoxically, at the same time that she revives her dead parents through memory, she distances herself from them by acknowledging their complexity as individuals and the complexity of their marriage. As she sees her parents as individuals compacted of both comedy and tragedy, love and betrayal, she moves toward seeing herself as an autonomous woman rather than as a daughter. She moves beyond the sort of protection that Woolf's Cam Ramsay seeks from her father: "Now I can go on thinking

---

29. Weston, "Eudora Welty's *The Optimist's Daughter*," 76; Williams, "Virginia Woolf's Rhetoric of Enclosure," 46; Welty, Foreword to *To the Lighthouse,* ix.

whatever I like, and I shan't fall over a precipice or be drowned, for there
he is, keeping his eye on me" (*TL*, 304). Laurel moves from her early
need to confide in her mother about Fay's abuse of her father to wishing
to protect her mother's privacy and integrity by burning the letters and
diaries she finds in her mother's desk. Both Laurel and Lily move beyond
needing a mother to a discovery of their own power and creativity.

The distance that Laurel travels can be measured by the difference
between her interpretation of her own marriage at the start of this section
and her reading of it at the section's close. Looking at her wedding pho-
tograph early in Part 3, Laurel thinks, "Her father had given it a silver
frame. (So had she. Her marriage had been one of magical ease, of *ease*—
of brevity and conclusion and all belonging to Chicago and not here)"
(*OD*, 143). Framing it thus in her memory, Laurel has restricted interpretation of her marriage and resisted alternative readings and reevalua-
tions. By the end of this section, however, she is finally free to grieve
over the brevity of the marriage and to see that brevity as a far greater
flaw than the betrayal and loss that pervaded her parents' marriage toward
the end of her mother's life:

> What would have been their end, then? Suppose their marriage had ended
> like her father and mother's? Or like her mother's father and mother's?
> Like—
> "Laurel! Laurel! Laurel!" Phil's voice cried.
> She wept for what happened to life.
> "I wanted it!" Phil cried. His voice rose with the wind in the night and
> went around the house and around the house. It became a roar. "I wanted
> it!" (*OD*, 181)

The grief Laurel experiences is accompanied by a return to feeling, a
return to life. "A flood of feeling" descends upon her, and the "deepest
spring in her heart had uncovered itself, and it began to flow again" (*OD*,
180–81). In the very moment that she returns to life, to a life that is not
numb, muted, and centered on emotional protection, Laurel "wept for
what happened to life" (*OD*, 181). Like Lily Briscoe, she discovers that
"empty it was not, but full to the brim" (*TL*, 285). Paradoxically, the
disembodied Phil is the catalyst for Laurel's return to a full, embodied

life: "Left bodiless and graveless of a death made of water and fire in a year long gone, Phil could still tell her of her life" (*OD*, 186–87).

Sally Wolff traces the diminishing role played by Phil Hand in Welty's revisions of the short story into the novel: "As the literal presence of Phil diminishes, he metaphorically looms larger, and as the description of his everyday life with Laurel and their domestic bliss are made more sketchy, Phil becomes more fully identified." Wolff concludes that these revisions transform the work from "a story about love to a novel about tragedy and death."[30] The result is a complex exploration of the shifting dynamics among love and loss, life and death, presence and absence, and comedy and tragedy.

In Part 4 of *The Optimist's Daughter*, the brief concluding section, Laurel McKelva Hand brings to completion and acts upon her vision of the previous night. Laurel has her vision in the form of her dream of confluence. Unlike *To the Lighthouse*, however, *The Optimist's Daughter* goes on beyond the vision, putting it to the test in Laurel's confrontation with Fay.

Part 4 opens with a "textual" recovery of Phil Hand who, unlike her father, "was not an optimist" (*OD*, 188). Phil had the ability to live fully in the world, accepting both its gifts and its sorrows, without the denial of Clinton McKelva or the sense of betrayal of Becky McKelva: "Phil had learned everything he could manage to learn, and done as much as he had time for, to design houses to stand, to last, to be lived in; but he had known they could equally well, with the same devotion and tireless effort, be built of cards" (*OD*, 188).

Laurel's vision of confluence, born out of her memory of Phil, is challenged first by her encounter with the carnivalesque Mr. Cheek, who blunders through the house, chasing the entrapped bird from room to room, and then by her meeting with Fay. Laurel sees in Fay's desecration of her mother's breadboard, lovingly crafted by Phil, a tangible symbol of the present's constant betrayal of the past, in the same way that she felt the stories at the funeral violated her dead father. But her nighttime revelation prevails as she realizes that the past and living memory of the past are not the same:

---

30. Wolff, "Among Those Missing," 74–75.

The past is no more open to help or hurt than was Father in his coffin. The past is like him, impervious, and can never be awakened. It is memory that is the somnambulist. It will come back in its wounds from across the world, like Phil, calling us by our names and demanding its rightful tears. It will never be impervious. The memory can be hurt, time and again—but in that may lie its final mercy. As long as it's vulnerable to the living moment, it lives for us, and while it lives, and while we are able, we can give it up its due. (*OD*, 207)

Awakened by memory into feeling, Laurel is no longer remote and detached. Her return to feeling gives her the anger to almost hurt Fay, the compassion to relent, and the awareness that Fay "could no more fight a feeling person than she could love him" (*OD*, 206). In her final meeting with Fay, Laurel discovers that fulfillment, synthesis, and balance reside in her own self, not in her family home nor in the breadboard that Phil made and her mother used. She has learned that "memory lived not in initial possession but in the freed hands, pardoned and freed, and in the heart that can empty but fill again" (*OD*, 207–208).

THE ARTIST'S VISION

The need to mediate between two extremes, two oppositions, becomes an essential part of the structure of *To the Lighthouse* and *The Optimist's Daughter* as elegy is made to incorporate questioning and even criticism of the dead. Though the living may continue to love the dead, the dead do not offer a pattern for the living to follow. The novels establish extremes and oppositions that Lily Briscoe and Laurel McKelva Hand must address and somehow reconcile. As Laurel notes in thinking of her father's illness, the rivalry does not lie "between the living and the dead, between the old wife and the new; it's between too much love and too little" (*OD*, 178). The list of oppositions at work in each novel is extensive: presence/absence, life/death, optimism/pessimism, masculine/feminine, protection/violation. The novels avoid affirming one side of the oppositions at the expense of the other side. Rather, what Virginia Woolf and Eudora Welty face is the challenge of maintaining an awareness of the dynamic between the two sides of each opposition.

Carolyn Heilbrun argues against the critical perspective that advocates Mrs. Ramsay's perspective as *To the Lighthouse*'s privileged philosophy. She disagrees with the critical claim that because "Virginia Woolf is 'feminine,' we are to assume that she is championing the 'feminine' vision of Mrs. Ramsay against the life-denying 'masculine' vision of Mr. Ramsay." Heilbrun continues, "It has often been noticed that this masculine ordering of the world is deficient, and most readers and critics suppose Woolf to be condemning her father, or Mr. Ramsay, for this 'masculine' order while exalting the 'feminine' order of Mrs. Ramsay. But surely, if his division of truth into so artificial an order as the alphabet is life-denying, no less so is her moody and dreamy mistiness which, unable to distinguish objects on the sea, comparing itself to a wedge of darkness, demands the protection of men while undermining what truths they find." Judy Little agrees: "Neither of the clusters of imagery and value— the cluster of masculine imagery associated with Mr. Ramsay and the cluster of feminine imagery associated with Mrs. Ramsay—receives an endorsement in the novel's action."[31] Rather than supporting one side or the other, Woolf adopts a third alternative, a vision of the two modes as dependent upon each other.

Judge and Becky McKelva establish related poles of opposition in *The Optimist's Daughter*. Michael Kreyling has noted some of the similarities between Mr. Ramsay's masculine order and Judge McKelva's approach to the world. He argues that though Mr. Ramsay is "more thin-skinned than the judge," each man "faces the world armed with logic and 'laws.'" Both men, according to Kreyling, "cling to the realm of the abstract concept for meaning and stability in life. And they are both wrung by the horror of reaching some unfinished point, the letter Q, beyond which their powers cannot take them."[32] Similarities exist as well between Mrs. Ramsay and Becky. Each has the power to make of an everyday feminine activity—presiding over a dinner party, dying cloth, making a shirt, baking bread—an act of creative triumph. And the strain of feminine pessimism that causes Mrs. Ramsay to wish that her children

31. Heilbrun, *Toward a Recognition of Androgyny*, 76; Little, *Comedy and the Woman Writer*, 57.

32. Kreyling, *Eudora Welty's Achievement of Order*, 160–61.

need never grow up colors the painful descriptions of Becky's illness. Even more than Woolf's Mrs. Ramsay, Becky McKelva holds a vision of life that demands an uncompromising acknowledgment of limitation, death, and betrayal.

The conflict between the masculine and feminine perspectives is dramatized in the battle over Becky's illness. Whereas the Judge seeks to ignore her suffering, Becky reduces the meaning of her life and of her husband's and daughter's lives to pain and betrayal: "He loved his wife. Whatever she did that she couldn't help doing was all right. But it was *not* all right! Her trouble was that very desperation. And no one had the power to cause that except the one she desperately loved, who refused to consider that she was desperate. It was betrayal on betrayal" (*OD,* 176). John F. Desmond summarizes the shortcomings of the Judge's and Becky's different approaches to life:

> [Laurel] judges the failings of the mourners severely, as indeed Becky would have, and one of the ironies of the novel is that it is the mother and daughter who have judgmental vision, not the doting Clinton McKelva. Though we may fault the Judge's doting optimism, it is also important to see Welty's criticism of the judgmental vision of Becky and the Laurel of the earlier sections of the novel. Judging in its severest form represents an attempt to narrow and fix reality, a reduction of mystery which can be as life-denying as doting. In short, doting and judging are opposite extremes of vision, both distortive insofar as they attempt to impose a fixed pattern on the fluid mystery of reality.[33]

Like Woolf in *To the Lighthouse,* Welty does not champion one of these perspectives over the other, but seeks a third, dynamic alternative.

The third alternative suggested by Woolf in *To the Lighthouse* and Welty in *The Optimist's Daughter* takes form in the artist figure. Both Lily Briscoe and Laurel McKelva Hand are artists, and the similarities between the two are striking. Laurel is forty in Welty's novel; Lily is forty-four in

33. John F. Desmond, "Pattern and Vision in *The Optimist's Daughter,*" in *A Still Moment: Essays on the Art of Eudora Welty,* ed. John F. Desmond (Metuchen, N.J., 1978), 126.

"The Lighthouse" section of Woolf's novel. Lily is a spinster; Laurel is a widow. Neither has the responsibilities of wife and/or mother that might intrude upon her dedication to her art.[34] This freedom releases Lily and Laurel from one of the primary dilemmas of the artist heroine that Linda Huf describes in *A Portrait of the Artist as a Young Woman:* "She is torn . . . between her role as a woman, demanding selfless devotion to others, and her aspirations as an artist, requiring exclusive commitment to work. Unlike the artist hero she must choose between her sexuality and her profession, between her womanhood and her work."[35]

Despite this essential freedom, each of these artists must struggle with her society's expectations of her; in neither case do these expectations include a devotion to art. The choices and challenges facing a woman artist differ radically from those facing a male artist. As Leslie Hankins writes, "The question 'Will I be an artist or a banker?' is a much different question from 'Will I be an artist or a woman?' and it is the latter question which haunts aspiring women artists from Lily Briscoe in Virginia Woolf's *To the Lighthouse* to those in Welty's work."[36] Mrs. Ramsay pressures Lily to marry, and Charles Tansley subjects her to his litany of "women 'can't paint, can't write'" (*TL*, 137). Mount Salus views Laurel's decision to pursue her career as a form of betrayal. Parodying the Mount Salus view, Fay tells her, "Oh, I wouldn't have run off and left anybody that needed me. Just to call myself an artist and make a lot of money" (*OD*, 37). After the funeral, the women of Mount Salus try to persuade Laurel to give up her career as an artist and to stay in Mount Salus, to assume her mother's role in the town. "Who's going to kill you if you don't draw those pictures?" asks Miss Tennyson. "As I was saying to Tish,

34. It is interesting to note that both Virginia Woolf and Eudora Welty were similarly free to pursue their own artistic careers. Neither had children, and though Woolf was married, her marriage to Leonard Woolf was one that fostered rather than hindered her writing. Both women did, however, find that their roles as daughters complicated their writing careers. Woolf's difficulties were primarily psychological; for Welty, the years she spent nursing her mother in a final illness were not productive in terms of her literary career.

35. Linda Huf, *A Portrait of the Artist as a Young Woman: The Writer as Heroine in American Literature* (New York, 1983), 5.

36. Hankins, "Alas, Alack! Or a Lass, a Lack?" 394.

'Tish, if Laurel would stay home and Adele would retire, we could have as tough a bridge foursome as we had when Becky was playing'" (*OD*, 133–34).

Finally, both are visual artists: Lily paints, and Laurel designs fabrics. Laurel's artistic medium is especially interesting because of its linguistic connection to writing; textile and textuality come from the same Latin root meaning "to weave." As Ruth Weston points out, Laurel's medium is part of her maternal inheritance: "Becky herself is seen as an artist in words and fabric, connecting women's writing with domestic arts." The choice of visual arts is closely tied to the theme of vision and perception in each novel and stresses the importance of vision, of how one sees in art or in life. Speaking of Cassie Morrison, another of Welty's female artist figures, Louis D. Rubin, Jr., says that she "possesses the vision that understands what lies in and under the surfaces of her experience without at the same time being so driven and distracted by that knowledge that she cannot live in a place." [37] This passage could easily describe Lily Briscoe, the single character in *To the Lighthouse* whose vision encompasses the other characters, who can see past her own needs and desires into the nature of others. Her painting of Mrs. Ramsay captures not her beautiful features, but represents Mrs. Ramsay's unspoken sense of herself as "a wedge-shaped core of darkness" (*TL*, 95). The last line of Woolf's novel, "I have had my vision" (*TL*, 310), stresses the connection between art and perception.

Rubin's comment also describes the sort of artist that Laurel becomes by the end of her novel. Eyes and vision are important motifs in *The Optimist's Daughter*, from the opening pages when Judge McKelva travels to New Orleans to see Dr. Courtland because he feels there is "something wrong with my *eyes*" (*OD*, 10). One of the working titles for *The Optimist's Daughter* was "Poor Eyes," and throughout the opening pages, words relating to vision are italicized, visually stressing the importance of vision and perception. [38] Both of Laurel's parents eventually lose their

37. Weston, "Eudora Welty's *The Optimist's Daughter*," 86; Rubin, *A Gallery of Southerners*, 65.

38. Wolff, "Among Those Missing," 81, recounts Welty's humorous remarks about the title: "I wanted to have something about the eyes. I first wanted to call it 'Poor Eyes,' but that was voted down. Bill Maxwell and Diarmuid Russell didn't like it. Bill did like

physical vision. Laurel's struggle, though she does not realize it till late in the novel, is to recover and sustain her own vision, her ability to distinguish and understand the patterns at work in her own life. The final sentence of *The Optimist's Daughter* connects the novel's patterns of eyes and hands, the two primary tools of the visual artist. As she leaves Mount Salus, "the last thing Laurel *saw,* before they whirled into speed, was the twinkling of their *hands,* the many small and unknown hands, wishing her goodbye" (*OD,* 208; emphasis added).

The hand images refer as well to Laurel's husband, Phil Hand, who "taught her to draw, to work toward and into her pattern, not to sketch peripheries" (*OD,* 188). Welty's novel is structured on much the same principle of working into its patterns. As Laurel learns to discern the patterns in her experience, the novel develops its own patterns of meaning. Patterning becomes a means of creating form and meaning, of calling forth order from chaos. In one of her memories from early childhood, Laurel recalls sitting on the floor of the sewing room and playing with the scraps of cloth left over from her mother's sewing, forming them "into stars, flowers, birds, people, or whatever she liked to call them, lining them up, spacing them out, making them into patterns, families, on the sweet-smelling matting" (*OD,* 159). It is this sort of patterning that forms Laurel's work as a designer of fabrics, this sort of patterning that Laurel must learn to do in her life, and this sort of patterning that Welty uses to give coherence and meaning to her novel. John Desmond claims that the most important pattern in *The Optimist's Daughter* "has to do with images of patterns themselves, images of ordering, seen for example in Laurel's career as a designer of fabrics, in her mother's love of sewing, in Phil's career as a designer and maker, and most importantly, in the very acts of reflection and memory, themselves faculties for ordering perception and experience." Noting that in earlier drafts Welty represented Laurel as a painter rather than a designer of fabrics, Sally Wolff comments, "As an architect, Phil imagines and sketches houses—

The Optimist's Daughter. . . . After the book came out I had letters that had the title wrong: 'I so much enjoyed *The Optimistic Daughter.*' Another said *The Optometrist's Daughter.* That's a good one, don't you think? The Optometrist's Daughter? Because of the eyes?"

domestic structures—while Laurel, first a painter, later opts for design—
she becomes a decorator of interior spaces. This change in Laurel's career,
from painter to interior designer, is a significant one, suggesting that she
is a shaper of interior landscapes."[39] Although in the novel Laurel is
described as "a professional designer of fabrics" (OD, 25) rather than an
interior designer, Wolff's emphasis on interiority and design is apt. Patterning becomes a means of creating form and meaning.

In Woolf's novel Lily Briscoe connects this process with love: "Love
had a thousand shapes. There might be lovers whose gift it was to choose
out the elements of things and place them together and so, giving them
a wholeness not theirs in life, make of some scene, or meeting of people
(all now gone and separate), one of those globed compacted things over
which thought lingers, and love plays" (TL, 286). As Laurel, too, learns,
"her life, any life . . . was nothing but the continuity of its love" (OD,
187). The artist in Welty's novel, like the lover, does not merely see the
meaning in events or objects, but through seeing *creates* alternative narratives and meanings. The artist is one who negotiates meaning in the
context of the human relationships of marriages, families, and communities. It is this interpretation of the artist of Woolf's novel that Welty
comments on in her foreword:

> Set down here in the surround of the sea, on the spinning earth, caught up
> in the mysteries and the threat of time, the characters in their separate ways
> are absorbed in the wresting of order and sequence out of chaos, of shape
> out of what shifts and changes or vanishes before their eyes. The act of
> thinking, the act of using a brush dipped in greens and blues to set down
> "what I see" on a square of paper, the giving of human love, of making the
> moment something permanent, are all responses made at great risk ("risk"
> is the novel's repeated word) to the same question, "What does it all mean?"[40]

When, as in an autobiographical novel, the artist's subject matter is
her own experience, art is intimately connected to memory. Lily com-

39. Desmond, "Pattern and Vision in *The Optimist's Daughter*," in *A Still Moment*,
ed. Desmond, 119; Wolff, "Among Those Missing," 80.

40. Welty, Foreword to *To the Lighthouse*, xi.

ments on her memory of a day at the beach with Mrs. Ramsay that "stayed in the mind affecting one almost like a work of art" (*TL*, 240). Her reconciling vision at the novel's end both depends on her memory of Mrs. Ramsay and has the power to recall Mrs. Ramsay from the dead; in fact, Lily's painting represents the memory of another, earlier painting that she did not get to finish. Speaking of this connection between memory and art, DiBattista says, "The Woolfian artist is the spiritual medium that mediates between the living and the dead on the hallowed ground where death and life intersect. Her act, hovering in the fictional space . . . between mimesis and invocation, is a summoning of ancestral ghosts."[41] The Weltian artist is even more fully an artist of memory. The most beautiful and meaningful image that Laurel McKelva Hand creates comes from memory and summons a ghost: her dream of confluence based on her train ride with Phil. In this image, most of the patterns developed throughout the novel merge into a single, significant image of "sky, water, birds, light, and confluence" (*OD*, 186). As Laurel discovers, meaning resides in "the patterns restored by dreams" (*OD*, 208). Welty ends her literary autobiography, *One Writer's Beginnings,* with the same image of confluence: "Of course the greatest confluence of all is that which makes up the human memory—the individual human memory. My own is the treasure most dearly regarded by me, in my life and in my work as a writer" (*OWB*, 104).

41. DiBattista, *The Fables of Anon,* 67.

ORALITY, TEXTUALITY, AND PLEASURE

I N a 1980 interview with Joanna Maclay, Welty quotes the novelist Henry Green to describe both herself as a reader and her imagined ideal reader: "Prose should be a long intimacy between strangers with no direct appeal to what both have known. It should slowly appeal to feelings unexpressed, it should in the end draw tears out of the stone" (*C*, 282). Eudora Welty's interaction with Virginia Woolf's fiction has been just that—"a long intimacy between strangers" that continues on. Describing her experience of rereading *To the Lighthouse* in 1981, in order to write her foreword to that novel, Welty reveals that Woolf's fiction has continued to affect her as both a reader and a writer:

> That feeling of discovery you get with such a novel is the most marvelous thing. A door has been opened. I've just now been trying to write about Virginia Woolf's novel *To the Lighthouse*. Harcourt Brace is getting out a new edition of three of her novels, and they're having a living woman writer to write a little foreword for each; just sort of what it means to you. So I'm doing the one that meant the most to me which was *To the Lighthouse*. I've been trying to describe that feeling you get when you come upon something. I came upon it absolutely cold and it just knocked me out. I've read it lots of times since, but I read it again in order to write this piece, and it did the same thing. (*C*, 324–25)

"I think always I loved writing because I loved reading," claims Welty

(*C,* 175). This study has explored the ways in which Welty's reading and rereading of one particular author contributed to the writer she has become.

The image of oral pleasure—the "sweet devouring" that is the title of one of Welty's essays about reading and that I used to begin this study—is a valuable metaphor for thinking about the sort of revolutionary writing by women that is found in the fiction of Woolf and Welty. Welty carries the metaphor of devouring through that essay, writing of "gobbl[ing] up installment after installment" of a children's book (*E,* 282) and of her early need of "more to read than [she] *could* read" (*E,* 281). Elsewhere, she describes herself as "a ferocious, voracious reader" (*C,* 174) with "an enormous appetite for reading" (*C,* 143). In *Losing Battles,* Miss Julia Mortimer is described as writing "with her tongue spreading out . . . like words, just words, was getting to be something good enough to eat. And nothing else was!" (*LB,* 272).

"What is Reading?" asks Hélène Cixous. "It's Eating on the Sly." In Bakhtin's *Rabelais,* images of eating, of banqueting, are "intimately connected with speech" and the body's "interaction with the world . . . [in which] the body transgresses . . . its own limits: it swallows, devours, rends the world apart, is enriched and grows at the world's expense." Bakhtin goes on to characterize this interaction as a powerful and creative one: this "encounter with the world in the act of eating is joyful, triumphant; man triumphs over the world, devours it without being devoured himself." [1] Welty has indeed devoured Woolf's writing, and her fiction is "enriched" through this "transgress[ion of] its own limits." In addition, the novels in this study devour other genres in acts of enriching transgression and appropriation.

The phrase "sweet devouring" could be used to describe two scenes from Welty's fiction in which eating becomes a metaphor for a woman's joyous rejection of patriarchal values. In the first scene, from the novel *Delta Wedding,* the bride-to-be, Dabney, goes out for an early-morning excursion on the day of the wedding rehearsal. "She had even come out without her breakfast, having eaten only what was in the kitchen, milk

1. Hélène Cixous, *Three Steps on the Ladder of Writing,* trans. Sarah Cornell and Susan Sellers (New York, 1993), 21; Bakhtin, *Rabelais and His World,* 281.

and biscuits and a bit of ham and a chicken wing, and a row of plums sitting in the window" (*DW,* 120). She rides her "little filly" through a landscape of rich, ripe imagery in which fences, typically images of limitation and constraint, are transformed into sources of pleasure and nourishment: "The occasional fences smelled sweet, their darkened wood swollen with night dew like sap, and following her progress the bayou rustled within, ticked and cried. The sky was softly blue all over, the last rim of sunrise cloud melting into it like the foam on fresh milk" (*DW,* 120). In the course of this morning ride, Dabney recalls and rejects the southern and familial legends of "honor, honor, honor" (*DW,* 120) that led to the death of her grandfather in a duel over cotton. In response to this legend, Dabney thinks, "All the cotton in the world was not worth one moment of life! . . . How sweet life was, and how well she could hold it, pluck it, eat it, lay her cheek to it—oh, no one else knew. The juice of life and the hot, delighting taste and the fragrance and warmth to the cheek, the mouth" (*DW,* 120–21). After a scene of ravenous eating and landscape images transformed to food, life itself is imaged as a fruit that Dabney devours with sensuous pleasure in the same moment that she manages to step outside of her familial and cultural narratives to imagine alternative values and lives.

In the second scene, from the story "June Recital," Welty uses the sensual imagery of food to celebrate a woman's possession and enjoyment of her own sexuality. As Virgie and a sailor indulge in playful, abandoned sex, the narrator's description of the ripe figs hanging from the tree outside the window of their room provides a language for the expression of Virgie's pleasure: "They were rusty old fig trees but the figs were the little sweet blue. When they cracked open their pink and golden flesh would show, their inside flowers and golden bubbles of juice would hang, to touch your tongue to first" (*GA,* 21). In the rich, sensual, sexually charged language of this passage, Virgie's sexual pleasure is transformed into Welty's textual pleasure. Orality is thus a metaphor not just for reading as a woman but for writing as a woman.[2]

"To go honey mad," explains Patricia Yaeger, "is to go language mad"

---

2. Suzan Harrison, "The Other Way to Live: Gender and Selfhood in *Delta Wedding* and *The Golden Apples,*" *Mississippi Quarterly,* XLIV (1990–91), 62.

and to indulge in "the possession of a delicious excess of meaning that is forbidden, but therefore twice delicious." What we see in the novels of Woolf and Welty is what Yaeger calls the "poetics of excess," a poetics that Hélène Cixous begins to map out in "Laugh of the Medusa": "That which is ours breaks loose from us without our fearing any debilitation. Our glances, our smiles, are spent; laughs exude from our mouths; our blood flows and we extend ourselves without ever reaching an end."[3] By using language play, rich, excessive imagery, and nonlinear narrative structures, by decentering narrative authority, and by surprising the reader by undercutting expectations based on generic forms, Woolf and Welty exploit the possibilities of language to articulate feminine pleasure.

In *Honey-Mad Women*, Yaeger uses Bakhtin's ideas of banqueting and orality to suggest ways of recognizing and theorizing "the woman writer's oral victories." Yaeger argues that in feminist theory's emphasis on language as oppressive to women, "we tend to ignore the woman writer's double orality—her capacity for transforming boundaries, for defining her own loci of power." She devotes her critical study of women's writing to mapping out a countertradition that recognizes the emancipatory strategies that women writers have created: "As we define a counter tradition in women's writing and set beside the metaphors that tell us language is the medium of woman's oppression and suffering, images of women who seize words and use them for their own purposes, these new images can help us focus on those pleasurable, powerful aspects of women's reality we have hitherto neglected. We need to allow our critical practices to foreground the woman writer's ability to redefine her own marginality—to revise her banishment to the borders of culture."[4] This study has examined some of the strategies for redefinition and revision—some of the oral victories—that Woolf's fiction modeled for Welty in her development as a writer.

I have suggested that Woolf and Welty make use of what Bakhtin calls the novel's dialogism in a variety of ways. Bakhtin's concept of a dialogic helps to define a literary relationship between two women writers, a definition that differs from the traditional paradigms of influence as imi-

---

3. Yaeger, *Honey-Mad Women*, 28, 21; Cixous, "The Laugh of the Medusa," 336.
4. Yaeger, *Honey-Mad Women*, 4, 5, 6–7.

tation. Describing influence as the appropriation of and response to another's discourse, Bakhtin writes, "When such influences are laid bare, the half-concealed life lived by another's discourse is revealed within the new context of the given author. When such an influence is deep and productive, there is no external imitation, no simple act of reproduction, but rather a further creative development of another's (more precisely, half-other) discourse in a new context and under new conditions."[5] By laying bare the traces of Woolf's discourse in Welty's fiction, I have sought to demonstrate some of Welty's developing subtlety, skill, and vision as a writer. The great difference between the relationship of *To the Lighthouse* to *Delta Wedding* and to *The Optimist's Daughter* shows that as Welty moved more confidently into her own vision, her response to Woolf's fiction became less direct, and more productive and mature.

Speaking of Woolf's achievement as a writer, Welty gives her the highest praise: "It is an exertion, a vaunting, a triumph of wonder, of imaginative speculation and defiance; it is that bolt of lightning Virginia Woolf began with, an instantaneous burst of coherence over chaos and the dark. She has shown us the shape of the human spirit."[6] For Welty, too, writing involves wonder and defiance, "exposing yourself to risk" (*OWB*, 101) and "serious daring" (*OWB*, 104). It also involves what Welty calls *confluence*, "one of the chief patterns of human experience" (*OWB*, 102), and a metaphor of Welty's own that describes the fruitful relationship between these two writers. "It is our inward journey," says Welty, "that leads us through time—forward or back, seldom in a straight line, most often spiraling. Each of us is moving, changing, with respect to others. As we discover, we remember; remembering, we discover; and most intensely do we experience this when our separate journeys converge. Our living experience at those meeting points is one of the charged dramatic fields of fiction" (*OWB*, 102). The meeting point of Virginia Woolf's fiction and Eudora Welty's imagination has resulted in a body of fiction that provides many a sweet devouring for other voracious readers.

5. Bakhtin, *The Dialogic Imagination,* 347.
6. Welty, Foreword to *To the Lighthouse,* xii.

BIBLIOGRAPHY

Abel, Elizabeth. *Virginia Woolf and the Fictions of Psychoanalysis.* Chicago, 1989.

Appel, Alfred, Jr. *A Season of Dreams: The Fiction of Eudora Welty.* Baton Rouge, 1965.

Apuleius. *The Golden Ass.* Translated by Robert Graves. New York, 1951.

Bakhtin, Mikhail. *The Dialogic Imagination: Four Essays.* Edited by Michael Holquist. Translated by Caryl Emerson and Michael Holquist. Austin, 1981.

———. *Rabelais and His World.* Translated by Helene Iswolsky. Bloomington, 1984.

Bakker, Jan. *Pastoral in Antebellum Southern Romance.* Baton Rouge, 1989.

Bass, Eben E. "The Languages of *Losing Battles.*" *Studies in American Fiction,* XXI (Spring, 1993), 67–82.

Bauer, Dale M. *Feminist Dialogics: A Theory of Failed Community.* Albany, 1988.

Bauer, Dale M., and Susan Jaret McKinstry. *Feminism, Bakhtin, and the Dialogic.* Albany, 1991.

Beauvoir, Simone de. *The Second Sex.* Translated and edited by H. M. Parshley. 1953; rpr. New York, 1974.

Bloom, Harold. *The Anxiety of Influence: A Theory of Poetry.* Oxford, 1973.

Boatwright, James. "Speech and Silence in *Losing Battles.*" *Shenandoah,* XXV (Spring, 1974), 3–14.

Booth, Wayne C. "Freedom of Interpretation: Bakhtin and the Challenge of Feminist Criticism." *Critical Inquiry,* IX (1982), 45–76.

Brantley, Will. *Feminine Sense in Southern Memoir: Smith, Glasgow, Welty, Hellman, Porter, and Hurston.* Jackson, 1993.

Brinkmeyer, Robert H., Jr. "New Orleans, Mardi Gras, and Eudora Welty's *The Optimist's Daughter.*" *Mississippi Quarterly,* XLIV (1991), 429–41.

Brown, Ashley. "Eudora Welty and the Mythos of Summer." *Shenandoah,* XX (Spring, 1969), 29–35.

Burns, Christy L. "Re-Dressing Feminist Identities: Tensions Between Essential and Constructed Selves in Virginia Woolf's *Orlando.*" *Twentieth-Century Literature,* XL (1994), 342–64.

Carson, Barbara Harrell. "Eudora Welty's Dance with Darkness: *The Robber Bridegroom.*" *Southern Literary Journal,* XX (1988), 51–68.

―――. *Eudora Welty: Two Pictures at Once in Her Frame.* Troy, N.Y., 1992.

Caughie, Pamela L. *Virginia Woolf and Postmodernism.* Urbana, 1991.

Chamlee, Kenneth D. "Grimm and Apuleius: Myth-Blending in Eudora Welty's *The Robber Bridegroom.*" *Notes on Mississippi Writers,* XXIII (1991), 37–45.

Cixous, Hélène. "The Laugh of the Medusa." Translated by Keith Cohen and Paula Cohen. In *New French Feminisms,* edited by Elaine Marks and Isabelle de Courtivron. New York, 1981.

―――. *Three Steps on the Ladder of Writing.* Translated by Sarah Cornell and Susan Sellers. New York, 1993.

Derrida, Jacques. *Writing and Difference.* Translated by Alan Bass. Chicago, 1978.

Desmond, John F., ed. *A Still Moment: Essays on the Art of Eudora Welty.* Metuchen, N.J., 1978.

Devlin, Albert J. *Eudora Welty's Chronicle: A Story of Mississippi Life.* Jackson, 1983.

―――. "Modernity and the Literary Plantation: Eudora Welty's *Delta Wedding.*" *Mississippi Quarterly,* XLIII (1990), 163–72.

―――, ed. *Welty: A Life in Literature.* Jackson, 1987.

DiBattista, Maria. *Virginia Woolf's Major Novels: The Fables of Anon.* New Haven, 1980.

DuPlessis, Rachel Blau. *Writing Beyond the Ending: Narrative Strategies of Twentieth-Century Women Writers.* Bloomington, 1985.

Felman, Shoshana. "Woman and Madness: The Critical Phallacy." *Diacritics,* V (Winter, 1975), 2–10.

Ferguson, Mary Anne. "The Female Novel of Development and the Myth of Psyche." *Denver Quarterly,* XVII (1983), 58–74.

Fuller, Danielle. "Making a Scene: Some Thoughts on Female Sexuality and Marriage in Eudora Welty's *Delta Wedding* and *The Optimist's Daughter.*" *Mississippi Quarterly,* XLVIII (1995), 291–318.

Gilbert, Sandra M., and Susan Gubar. *The Madwoman in the Attic: The Woman*

Writer and the Nineteenth-Century Literary Imagination. New Haven, 1979.

Gretlund, Jan Nordby. *Eudora Welty's Aesthetics of Place.* Newark, 1994.

Grimm, Jakob, and Wilhelm Grimm. *Grimms' Tales for Young and Old: The Complete Stories.* Translated by Ralph Manheim. New York, 1977.

Guiguet, Jean. *Virginia Woolf and Her Works.* Translated by Jean Stewart. New York, 1976.

Gygax, Franziska. *Serious Daring from Within: Female Narrative Strategies in Eudora Welty's Novels.* Westport, Conn., 1990.

Hankins, Leslie Kathleen. "Alas, Alack! Or a Lass, a Lack? Quarrels of Gender and Genre in the Revisionist *Kunstlerroman:* Eudora Welty's *The Golden Apples.*" *Mississippi Quarterly,* XLIV (1991), 391–409.

Hardy, John Edward. "*Delta Wedding* as Region and Symbol." *Sewanee Review,* LX (1952), 397–417.

Harper, Howard. *Between Language and Silence: The Novels of Virginia Woolf.* Baton Rouge, 1982.

Harrison, Elizabeth Jane. *Female Pastoral: Women Writers Re-Visioning the American South.* Knoxville, 1991.

Harrison, Suzan. "The Other Way to Live: Gender and Selfhood in *Delta Wedding* and *The Golden Apples.*" *Mississippi Quarterly,* XLIV (1990–91), 49–68.

Heilbrun, Carolyn. *Hamlet's Mother and Other Women.* New York, 1990.

———. *Toward a Recognition of Androgyny.* New York, 1973.

Homans, Margaret, ed. *Virginia Woolf: A Collection of Critical Essays.* Englewood Cliffs, N.J., 1993.

Huf, Linda. *A Portrait of the Artist as a Young Woman: The Writer as Heroine in American Literature.* New York, 1983.

Jacobus, Mary. *Reading Women: Essays in Feminist Criticism.* New York, 1986.

Kolodny, Annette. "A Map for Rereading: Gender and the Interpretation of Literary Texts." In *New Feminist Criticism: Essays on Women, Literature, and Theory,* edited by Elaine Showalter. New York, 1985.

Kreyling, Michael. *Author and Agent: Eudora Welty and Diarmuid Russell.* New York, 1991.

———. *Eudora Welty's Achievement of Order.* Baton Rouge, 1980.

Kristeva, Julia. "Phonetics, Phonology, and Impulsional Bases." Translated by Caren Greenberg. *Diacritics,* IV (Fall, 1974), 33–37.

Ladd, Barbara. "Coming Through: The Black Initiate in *Delta Wedding.*" *Mississippi Quarterly,* XLI (1988), 541–51.

Little, Judy. *Comedy and the Woman Writer: Woolf, Spark, and Feminism.* Lincoln, Nebr., 1983.

————. "(En)gendering Laughter: Woolf's *Orlando* as Contraband in the Age of Joyce." In *Last Laughs: Perspectives on Women and Comedy*, edited by Regina Barreca. New York, 1988.

Love, Jean. "*Orlando* and Its Genesis: Venturing and Experimenting in Art, Love, and Sex." In *Virginia Woolf: Revaluation and Continuity*, edited by Ralph Freedman. Berkeley, 1980.

Manning, Carol S., ed. *The Female Tradition in Southern Literature*. Urbana, 1993.

————. *With Ears Opening Like Morning Glories: Eudora Welty and the Love of Storytelling*. Westport, Conn., 1985.

Marcus, Jane. *Virginia Woolf and the Languages of Patriarchy*. Bloomington, 1987.

————, ed. *New Feminist Essays on Virginia Woolf*. Lincoln, Nebr., 1981.

Mark, Rebecca. *The Dragon's Blood: Feminist Intertextuality in Eudora Welty's "The Golden Apples."* Jackson, 1994.

Meese, Elizabeth A. *Crossing the Double Cross: The Practice of Feminist Criticism*. Chapel Hill, 1986.

Miller, Lisa K. "The Dark Side of Our Frontier Heritage: Eudora Welty's Use of the Turner Thesis in *The Robber Bridegroom*." *Notes on Mississippi Writers*, XIV (1981), 18–25.

Moi, Toril. *Sexual/Textual Politics*. New York, 1985.

Morson, Gary Saul. "Preface: Perhaps Bakhtin." In *Bakhtin: Essays and Dialogues on His Work,* edited by Gary Saul Morson. Chicago, 1986.

Mortimer, Gail. *Daughter of the Swan: Love and Knowledge in Eudora Welty's Fiction*. Athens, Ga., 1994.

Pollack, Harriet. "On Welty's Use of Allusion: Expectations and Their Revisions in 'The Wide Net,' *The Robber Bridegroom,* and 'At the Landing.'" *Southern Quarterly*, XXIX (1990), 5–32.

Porter, Katherine Anne. Collection. McKeldin Library, University of Maryland, Baltimore.

Prenshaw, Peggy Whitman, ed. *Conversations with Eudora Welty*. Jackson, 1984.

————, ed. *Eudora Welty: Critical Essays*. Jackson, 1979.

————. "Woman's World, Man's Place: The Fiction of Eudora Welty." In *Eudora Welty: A Form of Thanks,* edited by Louis Dollarhide and Ann J. Abadie. Jackson, 1979.

Randisi, Jennifer L. "Eudora Welty and the Fairy Tale." *Southern Literary Journal*, XIII (1990), 30–44.

Ransom, John Crowe. "Delta Fiction." *Kenyon Review*, VIII (1946), 503–507.

Romines, Ann. *The Home Plot: Women, Writing and Domestic Ritual*. Amherst, 1992.

Rubin, Louis D., Jr. *A Gallery of Southerners*. Baton Rouge, 1982.

————. "Everything Brought Out in the Open: Eudora Welty's *Losing Battles*." *Hollins Critic,* VII (Spring, 1970), 1–12.

————. *The Faraway Country: Writers of the Modern South.* Seattle, 1963.

Schmidt, Peter. *The Heart of the Story: Eudora Welty's Short Fiction.* Jackson, 1991.

Schweickart, Patrocinio P. "Reading Ourselves: Toward a Feminist Theory of Reading." In *Feminisms: An Anthology of Literary Theory and Criticism,* edited by Robyn R. Warhol and Diane Price Herndl. New Brunswick, N. J., 1991.

Simpson, Lewis P. *The Dispossessed Garden: Pastoral and History in Southern Literature.* Athens, Ga., 1975.

Slethaug, Gordon E. "Initiation in Eudora Welty's *The Robber Bridegroom.*" *Southern Humanities Review,* VII (1973), 77–87.

Sypher, Eileen B. "*The Waves:* A Utopia of Androgyny?" In *Virginia Woolf: Centennial Essays,* edited by Elaine K. Ginsberg and Laura Moss Gottlieb. Troy, N.Y., 1983.

Trautmann, Joanne. "*Orlando* and Vita Sackville-West." In *Critical Essays on Virginia Woolf,* edited by Morris Beja. Boston, 1985.

Trilling, Diana. "Fiction in Review." Review of Eudora Welty's *Delta Wedding. Nation,* May 11, 1946, p. 578.

Trilling, Lionel. "American Fairy Tale." *Nation,* December 19, 1942, p. 687.

Trouard, Dawn, ed. *Eudora Welty: The Eye of the Storyteller.* Kent, Ohio, 1989.

Turner, W. Craig, and Lee Emling Harding, eds. *Critical Essays on Eudora Welty.* Boston, 1989.

Vande Kieft, Ruth M. *Eudora Welty.* New York, 1962.

————. *Eudora Welty.* Rev. ed. Boston, 1987.

Warren, Robert Penn. "The Love and Separateness in Miss Welty." *Kenyon Review,* VI (1944), 246–59.

Watkins, Floyd C. "The Journey to Baltimore in *The Optimist's Daughter.*" *Mississippi Quarterly,* XXXVIII (1985), 435–40.

Welty, Eudora. *Delta Wedding.* New York, 1946.

————. *The Eye of the Story: Selected Essays and Reviews.* New York, 1978.

————. Foreword to *To the Lighthouse,* by Virginia Woolf. New York, 1981.

————. *The Golden Apples.* New York, 1949.

————. *Losing Battles.* New York, 1978. Vintage paperback.

————. "Mirrors for Reality." *New York Times Book Review,* April 16, 1944, p. 3.

————. *One Writer's Beginnings.* Cambridge, Mass., 1984.

————. *The Optimist's Daughter.* New York, 1978. Vintage paperback.

————. *The Robber Bridegroom.* 1942; rpr. New York, 1978.

Westling, Louise. "Food, Landscape and the Feminine in *Delta Wedding*." *Southern Quarterly*, XXX (1992), 29–40.

———. *Sacred Groves and Ravaged Gardens: The Fiction of Eudora Welty, Carson McCullers, and Flannery O'Connor*. Athens, Ga., 1985.

Weston, Ruth. "The Feminine and Feminist Texts of Eudora Welty's *The Optimist's Daughter*." *South Central Review*, IV (1987), 74–91.

———. *Gothic Traditions and Narrative Techniques in the Fiction of Eudora Welty*. Baton Rouge, 1994.

Williams, Carolyn. "Virginia Woolf's Rhetoric of Enclosure." *Denver Quarterly*, XVIII (1984), 43–61.

Wolff, Sally. "Among Those Missing: Phil Hand's Disappearance from *The Optimist's Daughter*." *Southern Literary Journal*, XXV (1992), 74–88.

Woolf, Virginia. *Collected Essays*. New York, 1925.

———. Review of *Revolving Lights*, by Dorothy Richardson. In *Women and Writing*, edited by Michele Barrett. New York, 1979.

———. *Orlando*. New York, 1928.

———. *A Room of One's Own*. New York, 1929.

———. *To the Lighthouse*. New York, 1927.

———. *The Waves*. New York, 1931.

———. *A Writer's Diary*. Edited by Leonard Woolf. New York, 1953.

Yaeger, Patricia. *Honey-Mad Women: Emancipatory Strategies in Women's Writing*. New York, 1988.

Zipes, Jack. *Fairy Tales and the Art of Subversion: The Classical Genre for Children and the Process of Civilization*. New York, 1983.

INDEX